THE BUSINESS OF PEOPLE

Leadership for the Changing World

THE BUSINESS OF PEOPLE

Leadership for the Changing World

Iain Fraser
Madeleine Taylor

CRC Press is an imprint of the
Taylor & Francis Group, an **informa** business

Herrmann Whole Brain (HBDI) is a registered trademark of Herrmann International.

PMI, *PMBOK® Guide*, and *Pulse of the Profession* are registered trademarks of the Project Management Institute, Inc., which is registered in the United States and other nations.

CRC Press
Taylor & Francis Group
6000 Broken Sound Parkway NW, Suite 300
Boca Raton, FL 33487-2742

© 2020 by Iain Fraser and Madeleine Taylor
CRC Press is an imprint of Taylor & Francis Group, an Informa business

No claim to original U.S. Government works

Printed on acid-free paper

International Standard Book Number-13: 978-0-367-25102-4 (Hardback)

This book contains information obtained from authentic and highly regarded sources. Reasonable efforts have been made to publish reliable data and information, but the author and publisher cannot assume responsibility for the validity of all materials or the consequences of their use. The authors and publishers have attempted to trace the copyright holders of all material reproduced in this publication and apologize to copyright holders if permission to publish in this form has not been obtained. If any copyright material has not been acknowledged please write and let us know so we may rectify in any future reprint.

Except as permitted under U.S. Copyright Law, no part of this book may be reprinted, reproduced, transmitted, or utilized in any form by any electronic, mechanical, or other means, now known or hereafter invented, including photocopying, microfilming, and recording, or in any information storage or retrieval system, without written permission from the publishers.

For permission to photocopy or use material electronically from this work, please access www.copyright.com (http://www.copyright.com/) or contact the Copyright Clearance Center, Inc. (CCC), 222 Rosewood Drive, Danvers, MA 01923, 978-750-8400. CCC is a not-for-profit organization that provides licenses and registration for a variety of users. For organizations that have been granted a photocopy license by the CCC, a separate system of payment has been arranged.

Trademark Notice: Product or corporate names may be trademarks or registered trademarks, and are used only for identification and explanation without intent to infringe.

Visit the Taylor & Francis Web site at
http://www.taylorandfrancis.com

and the CRC Press Web site at
http://www.crcpress.com

Early Reader Reviews

"In a world where leadership increasingly requires emotional and cultural intelligence skills, this masterpiece couldn't be any timelier. This must-read equips leaders with the ability to first understand themselves, and then use that understanding to lead others intentionally. This is a critical and missing piece in today's leadership space—you cannot give what you don't have. My key takeaway from this book is that effective leaders understand themselves, and are empathetic towards others."

Dr. Hilary Aza, Senior Portfolio Manager, Tarrant County

"The importance of leadership is now universally accepted as the critical capability for organisation success. Equally important is to understand oneself as an essential first step to be a great leader. This book offers guidance to support both, but most importantly provides a bridge between them in a very relatable and approachable way. This makes it essential for anyone seeking to better understand their personal leadership and to inform further development."

Rob Loader, Executive, Capital Planning & Delivery, Telstra Corporation

"A worthwhile read. A solid blend of neuroscience, psychology and business leadership theory, practice and tools. The authors Iain and Madeleine have created a book that is accessible to leaders both highly experienced and those entering leadership and management for the first time. The book to me is written from a position of empowerment, cultural acknowledgment, hopefulness and purpose."

Elissa Farrow, Founder, About Your Transition

"A certainty in life is change. To be successful leaders we must be able to change our own leadership style for the different situations we find ourselves in and the varied people we work with. Adaptability is a critical competency for great leaders. This book will challenge your own thinking and behaviour and give you an opportunity to develop your adaptability and leadership style for an evolving future."

Thomas Davis, GM, Corporate Services,
Capital & Coast District Health Board

If you've picked up this book, you likely have other leadership books on your shelf. THIS IS DIFFERENT. Imagine a playbook that guides you through leadership reflection, opportunity identification, then provides a path forward to an enlightened leadership needed in the VUCA-influenced world of today. Iain and Madeleine are honest and raw about the challenges faced, and the resiliency needed, to lead in business. They outline simple and REAL steps to demystify 'leadership'. This book acts as a guide to prepare you, and your teams, as you face the wicked problems of today—as leaders, as followers, and importantly, as people.

Suzanne M. O'Gorman, Senior Strategic Business
Architect, Innovation, United Healthcare National Accounts

Dedication

Hutia te rito o te harakeke, kei hea ra te komako eko?
Ki mai ki ahau, he aha te mea nui o te Ao?
Maku e ki atu, he tangata, he tangata, he tangata.

Maori proverb

If you were to pluck out the center of the flax bush, where would the bell bird sing?
If you were to ask me, "What is the most important thing in the world?"
I would reply, "It is the people, the people, the people."

Contents

Early Reader Reviews	*vii*
Dedication	*ix*
Contents	*xi*
List of Figures	*xv*
List of Tables and Tools	*xvii*
Foreword	*xix*
Acknowledgments	*xxi*
About the Authors	*xxiii*
Preface	*xxv*
Section One: Managing Yourself and Being the Best You Can Be	**1**
1.1 The Story So Far—Your Behavior Matters!	1
1.2 Case Study	2
1.2.1 The Importance of Soft Skills	3
1.3 Solutions for the Situation	4
1.3.1 Understanding How Your Brain Works	4
1.3.2 Increasing Your Self-Awareness	7
1.3.3 How Can You Change to Be the Best You Can Be?	15
1.3.4 Your Current Work Situation—An Awareness of the Pool in Which You Are Swimming	20
1.4 Case Study	26
1.5 Tools	26

xi

xii The Business of People: Leadership for the Changing World

Section Two: Leading Others One-on-One—Helping Others
Be the Best They Can Be   **37**

2.1   The Story So Far—Understanding and Working with Others   37

2.2   Case Study   38

2.3   Solutions for the Situation   39

    2.3.1   Setting Up for Success: Planning Your Interactions— Using Three Primary Negotiations   39

    2.3.2   Supporting People   47

    2.3.3   Daily Details and Corrections   55

2.4   Case Study—Using These Ideas for Success   61

2.5   Tools   61

Section Three: Managing Groups—Working Together for
Great Outcomes   **71**

3.1   The Story So Far—People Behave Consistently in Groups   71

3.2   Case Study   72

3.3   Solutions for the Situation   73

    3.3.1   Life Cycle of Groups   74

    3.3.2   Group Structures   80

    3.3.3   Group Dynamics   82

    3.3.4   Power Within a Group   87

    3.3.5   Dealing with Conflict   89

    3.3.6   Managing Group Processes   94

3.4   Case Study   99

3.5   Tools   100

Section Four: Leading the Organization—Creating a Dynamic
Organization Which Delivers Ongoing Value   **105**

4.1   The Story So Far—Building Organizational Competence   105

4.2   Case Study   107

4.3   Solutions for the Situation   108

    4.3.1   The 3P's to Success—Being Clear About What You Are Doing   108

    4.3.2   Culture—Delivering the Culture That Supports Your Vision   109

    4.3.3   Change, Change, Change   114

    4.3.4   Organizational Agility   121

    4.3.5   Organizational Sustainability   122

4.4   Case Study   124

4.5   Tools   126

Contents *xiii*

Epilogue	**133**
The Story Concludes	133
Appendix: Poems to Ponder	**137**
Glossary	**143**
Bibliography and References	**147**
Index	**153**

List of Figures

Figure 1.1	Grubs to Butterflies	17
Figure 1.2	STATE Tool	25
Figure 2.1	Ladder of Accountability	49
Figure 2.2	Ladder of Inference	54
Figure 2.3	Ego State Diagram	56
Figure 2.4	Continuum of Decision-Making Behavior	57
Figure 2.5	Skill/Will Matrix Diagram	60
Figure 3.1	Tuckman/Jensen Model with Project Stages	74
Figure 3.2	Building Blocks for Successful Teams	78
Figure 3.3	Four-Cornered Contract	79
Figure 3.4	Strong Matrix	81
Figure 3.5	Quadrant Perspectives	84
Figure 3.6	Drama Triangle	85
Figure 3.7	Winners' Triangle	86
Figure 3.8	Thomas-Kilmann Conflict Mode Instrument Model.	92
Figure 4.1	Change Types and Sustainability/Impact Relationship	116
Figure 4.2	Assessing Change Commitment	117

List of Tables and Tools

Table 3.1	Tuckman/Jensen Team Development Stages	77
Table 3.2	Positive versus Negative Conflict Recognition	89
Tool S1.1:	Focus Exercise	27
Tool S1.2:	Script Exercises	27
Tool S1.3:	Identity Conversation	28
Tool S1.4:	Identifying Feelings Worksheet	29
Tool S1.5:	Learning Style Preferences	30
Tool S1.6:	Working Styles	32
Tool S1.7:	Exploring Your Values	34
Tool S1.8:	Many Ways to Say "No"	36
Tool S1.9:	Assertiveness Tool	36
Tool S2.1:	Developing Trust—Time structuring	61
Tool S2.2:	Ladder of Accountability	62
Tool S2.3:	The 6 P's of Process—Process Preparation Sheet	63
Tool S2.4:	A Guide to Working with Me	64
Tool S2.5:	Basic Communication Skills Checklist	66
Tool S2.6:	Ladder of Inference.	69
Tool S3.1:	Circle Process	100
Tool S3.2:	Diversity Game	101
Tool S3.3:	Team Agreement/Charter	101

xvii

xviii   The Business of People: Leadership for the Changing World

Tool S3.4:	Kick-Off Meeting Run Sheet	102
Tool S3.5:	Facilitation Processes	103
Tool S3.6:	Problem-Solving and Decision-Making Tools	104
Tool S4.1:	Recognition Profile Datasheet	126
Tool S4.2:	Organization Assessment Questionnaire Sample	127
Tool S4.3:	Stakeholder Categorization Guide Sample	130
Tool S4.4:	Stakeholder Mapping Sample	131
Tool S4.5:	Communications Plan Sample	132

Foreword

I recall a conversation early in my career where a senior executive offered the notion that leadership was an elusive ideal. At that time, leadership as a formal competency was in its early stages. It seemed every other month, the covers of leading academic and business publications focused on leadership. Thought leaders such as Peter Drucker and Warren Bennis had already written several books on the topic, and organizations were beginning to use the notion in identification and selection of talent.

In that same period in my own organization, there was not much focus. We were highly successful. Exceptional growth and profitable performance. Shareholders were pleased. Yet the focus on leadership development at the executive level was a low priority, and for the broader management team and staff, a passing thought. I found myself spending personal time reading and immersing myself in the qualities and concepts that were portrayed on those front covers. That marked the beginning of my leadership journey, setting in motion the pursuit of understanding who I was and the leader I wanted to be. But I had to leave that organization to pursue it.

In Iain's book *The Business of Portfolio Management*,[*] he introduced us to the role of leadership in driving change in an organization. He highlighted that success in organizations depends on effective and relevant leadership. It's that simple. Leadership matters because the future is at greater risk without it. All strategic change happens through projects and programs, and projects and programs are led by people. The ability of an organization to change is therefore dependent on its people. It has been my lifelong assertion that people matter most. The tenants of strategy—competitive advantage, differentiation—are

---

[*] Fraser, 2017

created and sustained through people. This demands leadership from not only the top executives but from all levels.

Unfortunately, I still encounter far too many organizations, small and large, that fail to recognize the need to develop leadership. Many rely on a silver bullet approach, adopting the latest trend or buzzword, and failing to recognize the hard work required. This is especially true with people. I have never met anyone that has said they were motivated and inspired by process or technology, though necessary of course. Rather, they are motivated by a clearly articulated vision, trusting relationships, meaningful work where they can see how they are contributing to the vision, a boss that is invested in their success, respects their competence and allows them to succeed and fail.

Shifting from managing people to leading people requires a pivot. As you take on increasingly broader leadership roles you move from technical expertise and doing the work to enabling, motivating and supporting the work through others. You shift from having to be the person with the right answers to the person who can ask the right questions. And this shift is not necessarily natural and certainly not easy for all. It requires a conscious effort and more importantly a willingness to lead. That willingness is supported by a clear understanding of what leadership means personally, the set of values and principles you draw on, developing a mental model of the leader you want to be all based on who you are—and the dedication to its lifelong pursuit. It requires constant reflection and brutal honesty.

It requires one other thing too. Communication. Rolled into all of the profiles of leadership I have ever read is "excellent communications skills." Recent studies indicate individuals have less and less free time. With less time available it is likely that communications begin to slip in frequency and/or quality, and for the recipients they have less time to absorb and internalize. I had a conversation with the CEO of a global engineering company, and we discussed the value of communications as leaders and its role in driving change. He suggested that it used to be we need to communicate seven times for it to be effective, but it now feels more like a thousand times! Whatever the number, we know leaders are accountable to communicate and must invest in their ability as well as innovative ways to do so. Communication is an outcome, not an activity.

Regardless of where you are in your leadership journey, I am confident this new book from Madeleine and Iain will be a valuable resource for you. Enjoy the journey, it never ends . . .

Mark A. Langley
Former President/CEO
Project Management Institute

Acknowledgments

To our respective families, especially Britta and Wayne, who encouraged and supported us to pursue and complete this project.

To Taylor & Francis, our respected publishers, and John Wyzalek in particular, for the faith showed in accepting our proposal and the guidance that followed.

To Theron Shreve and Susan Culligan at DerryField Publishing Services for providing an outstanding function in getting our text to a readable stage.

A very special thank you to Mark Langley who graciously and expertly provided the Foreword and the deep insight and guidance it conveys.

Special thanks also to our early reviewers who gave their time and feedback comments on the early manuscript. Thank you Elissa, Hilary, Rob, Suzie, and Thomas.

To each of the leaders who have shared their thoughtful leadership quotes. Thanks to Craig, David, Jordon, Sarah, Scott F, Scott M, and Stew.

To our graphic designer Alastair Babbage for the great job done in translating our scribbles and creating our diagrams.

To Gabrielle and Sally for helping Madeleine speak what we wrote.

All the people Iain and Madeleine have worked with over the years and all the people who have supported their learning.

To the countless others around the world who helped shape our experiences, learnings, and views such that we could include in this content. Thank you.

About the Authors

Iain Fraser is somebody who truly understands the need for organizational change toward entities that are focused on developing their people to explore and deliver business value.

Iain has worked with and led teams around the world in the banking/finance, defense, engineering, government, oil & gas, power, and telecommunications sectors. Today he is a sought-after speaker, trusted advisor and trainer on business value and change.

Author of the top-selling business book *The Business of Portfolio Management—Boosting Organizational Value*[*] as well as over 25 other publications. He uses his 30+ years' professional and leadership experiences to craft his speaking, training, and mentoring activities.

His other passions and sources of joy are fly-fishing for trout and salmon, classic sports cars, and the making of hiking sticks. Playing good golf remains a challenge, however!

Tena koutou katoa,
Ko Mount Meredith te maunga,
Ko Whareama te awa,
Ko Ngati Pakeha te iwi,
No Beaumaris, Masterton ahau,
Ko Taylor toku whanau,
Ko Whangaui a Tara toku kainga anaienai
Ko Joe Taylor rāua ko Trish Taylor ōku mātua
Ko Wayne Ritani toko tane,
Ko Matt, Lorenzo, Guy taku tamariki
Ko Madeleine toku ingoa.

---

[*] Fraser, 2017

xxiv The Business of People: Leadership for the Changing World

Madeleine Taylor has worked with people on the forefront of trouble throughout her professional life, including mental and physical health, grief and loss, conflict and organizational challenges. Through that she has connected with people from many walks of life. Madeleine provides training, supervision, facilitation, and executive coaching. Of special interest for the past five years, Madeleine has been working with parents and educators about the impact of the overindulgent world on children and families. This has influenced her work with businesses.

In her spare time, she likes walking up hills, snow skiing, volunteering at the local surf club, and hanging out with friends and family.

Madeleine uses the pronouns she/her.

Preface

At the end of our life we may ask ourselves three questions:
Have I loved? Have I lived? Have I made a difference?

— Brendon Burchard[*]

Setting the Leadership Scene

We see that in the 21st century, a new type of leadership skill is required—one that is flexible, one that puts collaboration at the forefront, and yet one that requires individual courage to move at pace while balancing opportunity and risk. Above all, new leaders seek higher levels of value from all components of the modern organization. At the same time, there is a growing need to balance ethical behavior with the impact of overindulgence. Not easy in today's **V**olatile, **U**ncertain, **C**omplex and **A**mbiguous (VUCA) world, where speed of execution and the ability to change quickly will be the drivers of success.

In the book *The Business of Portfolio Management—Boosting Organizational Value,*[†] author Iain Fraser guided you to equip yourself and focus on business value through portfolio management. In that book for leaders, portfolio managers, program-of-work managers, and project leaders, Iain provided education, insight, and direction for what the Business of Portfolio Management is all about, with clear direction on approaches and tools to use to better the development of business strategy and its implementation. He offered and described the 3P's to

---

[*] www.actionpodcast.com/2012/08/brendon-burchards-three-questions-for-perspective-4827/

[†] Fraser, 2017

xxvi The Business of People: Leadership for the Changing World

Success (Purpose, People and Performance) as a philosophy for successful implementation and sustainability of a value-driven portfolio management approach.

This book is a sequel. It is purposefully focused on *people*. It comes with a unique mix of academic research and practical advice that is a differentiator from other books on leadership. The book will assist you to develop insight and grow your people leadership, knowledge, and skills. It is an opportunity to better manage yourself and lead others and your organization into the modern VUCA world.

International studies show that people are arriving into leadership roles with fewer soft-skill competencies than ever before, and those coming after them with even less.

Across the globe, from China through the Southeast Asian nations to the Americas and Europe and on through the Pacific Ocean, many people are arriving at work with the following characteristics: an inability to delay gratification, to need to always be the constant center of attention, to be disrespectful of people and property, to not know how much is enough, to be helpless and confused over wants and needs, to have an over-blown sense of entitlement, to be irresponsible, and to lack everyday skills (e.g., time keeping, focus). They are often ungrateful and have poor self-control, and this means they have relationship problems.

These are the characteristics of childhood overindulgence, as described in the book *How Much is Too Much?* by Clarke, Dawson, and Bredehoft.[*] Such employees are looking to their organizations to upskill them. Now, imagine that these people are moving into positions of leadership, where their personal goals are wealth, fame, and image. Somewhat scary, right?! Some are already there, and it might be you. (Check the set of characteristics above and see how many apply to you.)

Those with little soft-skill acumen have outcomes such as failed projects, dysfunctional teams, unresolved conflict within groups, or angst and churn within organizations because the people skills of the leaders, and thus their ability to lead, is lacking.

In your work, perhaps now but more so in the future, you will be required to create simplicity among increased complexity, make decisions with insufficient information, be nimble with time constraints, create opportunities where there are apparently none, act by your own notion of empowerment, and work with others who have vastly different understanding of behavior and ethics. All these situations require you to be at the top of your game as an individual and

---

[*] Clarke, Dawson, and Bredehoft, 2014

in a team environment. This is what the VUCA-influenced world will demand from you.

The content of this book will help you to:

- Understand yourself and how you impact others

- Enhance your interpersonal skills and build trust and empathy

- Evolve your flexibility

- Strengthen your skills for working with groups

- Expand your influencing capacity and refresh your conflict management strategies

- Grow your understanding of change management interventions

- Guide and lead teams and organizations

This book, however, is not a magic wand. It is designed to lead you to think about how your behavior matters in the daily interactions you have with others.

Before you carry on reading this book, we would like you to think about two aspects:

1. When you work with people and you are faced with problems, if you typically think (perhaps privately) that the problem is always caused by others, then you may not be ready to take on board what this book has to offer.

2. Know that in this book, people are "people." When people are referred to as resources, talent, full-time equivalent numbers, or pending retirees, they have been objectified. We want to acknowledge that people are human beings with lives that matter, as does yours.

If you relate to or practice the above beliefs and behaviors, we would recommend that you STOP right now and give this book to someone else, put it on the shelf, save it in your library, and go and live your life, perhaps get some coaching, until you are ready to comprehend that we all contribute to situations and that what is really important in our work is the people who make organizations work. No people—no work done.

In this book we acknowledge that you are a human being, and others are too, which means we are all fallible, make mistakes, and so contribute in some way to the problems we face. So come along with us as we provide insights, perspective, guidance, and practical tools that will assist you in learning about *The Business of People: Leadership for the Changing World.*

Our Values and Intentions

People matter, and we want to leave the planet in a condition to support those living on it many generations from now. We strive to be the best we can be. This book intends to share the experience and impacts that Madeleine and Iain have learned from real-world situations.

Iain's experience from working as a leader in and with multinational corporations, government organizations, and local businesses gives hands-on insights that will shape you as a leader and help you be the best you can be. His non-profit leadership experiences span the world.

Madeleine's experience of working with leaders, teams, and groups to manage difficult situations and transition to robust and fruitful outcomes will provide practical strategies to build a smoother path and, if used diligently, will prevent people-related issues from happening in the first place.

We understand that every person comes with their own valid frame of reference. We mean this to refer to the way each person understands the world. Their perceptions, thinking, and behavior are determined from their place on the planet, country, ethnicity, gender, birth order, schooling, and type of society they grew up in. This is the lens through which we see the world, and it helps to define us, others, and the world. It is not right or wrong, it just is. Mostly, how we understand the world is outside of our own awareness. This book will help you to learn about this often unspoken world that causes you to behave the way you do so.

Why do you need to be aware of your frame of reference? So that you will not be held hostage to those thinking habits if those habits are not serving you, or the people you work with, well. In addition, when your frame of reference fits with mine, then it is easy for us to work well and get along; however, if you have a different frame from me, then it is not so easy for either of us to see the world from each other's perspective.

What you might have noticed in reading this far could be an internal reaction to what we have said—often a response of confrontation or a desire to avoid. This is your frame of reference that has butted up against our frame of reference. Neither is right or wrong. If you are courageous enough to read on, please do so.

As authors we experienced this butting up against our frames of reference as we were working together on the book. Our personal frames of reference created a disconnect from time to time, which required lots of listening, acknowledgement of each other's right to hold their view, and robust discussion as we considered each other's view, vehemently argued our own perspective, and eventually agreed on the way forward. The result was a pragmatic one. Despite that, we

Preface *xxix*

laughed a lot and maintained our great respect for each other as people and the knowledge that we bring.

And now to our assumptions about people:

- We are all capable of learning.

- All behavior makes sense to the person exhibiting that behavior; no one gets out of bed intending to do a bad job (even the psychopaths among us!).

- We can choose our responses to every situation.

What this book will not do. It will not change your bad habits for you; you will have to put in some effort, but you can learn from the tools and case studies that we present. Leading people is an art and a science—you can read about the skills and tools, but you will need to practice them in order to finesse your art. That said, we have had to focus our approach and therefore have not detailed specifics about the wider mechanics of stakeholder and communications management.

So, start small and take one step and one idea at a time, be resilient, don't give up, stay underwhelmed, and yet be strong!

In order to get the most out of the book, we encourage you to give yourself time and space to reflect on what you are reading and dip in and out of the tools and exercises as you read through the book. This will help you to explore how the concepts might be playing out in your own leadership space.

Ronald Heifetz and Marty Linsky wrote in their book *Leadership on the Line: Staying Alive Through the Dangers of Leading** about the ability to observe ourselves. The analogy is of being in the dance or on the balcony: self, or whole picture. We have added a third perspective.

Imagine you are at a family wedding:

- Notice yourself as you dance on the dance floor.

- Notice the person/people you are dancing with and think about them.

- Imagine yourself on an elevated balcony being able to see it all—who is dancing with whom, what the bar staff are doing, who is kissing whom in the corner, who is unhappy, and how you are dancing.

From observing yourself in all three perspectives, you are more likely to see the situation as others might see it. And in addition, recognize that when you are in a tricky situation focused on the interaction, you may not always be able

---

* Heifetz and Linsky, 2002

to see everything, but taking time out (by going to the balcony) to reflect and observe can help you to lead with consideration.

Great leaders will give themselves the time and space for reflection. We aim to provoke that thinking. And of course, no amount of thinking will translate into action unless you take your thoughts and act on them.

How This Book Works

We provide practical concepts and tools that enable leaders of all types to work exceptionally well with people. Each section will have a repeating pattern:

a. There will be a **story** about a fictitious organization that embodies tales that Iain and Madeleine have heard over the years. The issues will be real, but the people and the organization will not. The story will illustrate the focus of that section of the book.

b. Specific topics focusing on key **solutions for the situation** in leading will be explained using concepts and research to build a clear understanding for you, the reader.

c. Real world **case studies**, albeit with names and places changed, that demonstrate the benefits of attending to what we are suggesting and the pitfalls of ignoring those messages.

d. A selection of **Tools** and situational guidance that will help you to reflect on your leadership practice and decide what options you have in any circumstance and how to act.

e. Throughout the book, we thread the following **themes**: sustainability, ethics, and the impact of overindulgence.

f. Selected **poems** to conclude.

The Story Begins

We begin by introducing Sam. (A gender-neutral name—notice those of you who have just sighed! This book is definitely for you. ☺) We have been thoughtful about the use of gender in the book. With increasing understanding of gender issues, we have decided to use a gender-neutral name for our main character and to change the gender as we work through the book. Section 1, They;

Section 2, She; Section 3, He; Section 4, gender neutral. Gender concerns and diversity are world-wide challenges that leaders of people need to confront and accommodate. So, we say more reason to read this book!

Sam has very good base skills—intelligence, personality, and positive drive. Sam works hard, has strong ethical behavior, and gets on well with people. A rising star! Sam is also a middle-distance running athlete with lots of resilience and determination. Recently, Sam has developed a passion for the design, assembly, and part-time racing of drones on a regional basis.

Sam works for an organization that desires to leverage the digital age for business advantage. The organization needs to change both its strategic direction and work habits to achieve the future the Board of Directors is looking for. The Board has placed urgency on this.

As the book progresses, Sam's story will raise real-world dilemmas for which the authors provide solutions for you to choose from and apply to your own real-world problems and challenges.

Section 1 focuses on Sam strengthening and building personal leadership competencies. Section 2 is about Sam supporting and working with individuals within a small team. Section 3 discusses Sam's role as a departmental manager, leading many teams; and Section 4 highlights Sam's transition to the role of CEO and leader of the organization.

Sam will need to work with a range of people in those different capacities as the leadership journey advances. Those include other leaders, subject matter experts, program-of-work and project teams, and organizational support staff such as human resource, finance, legal, IT, and marketing people.

One observation of Sam's career so far is that some skills need to be strengthened. Occasionally, Sam experiences a sense of being overwhelmed in the face of uncertainty, and this impacts Sam's ability to maintain an optimistic focus. Sam has a tendency to fall into criticizing others and being overly pedantic.

Read on and discover how Sam overcomes shortcomings, observes and addresses relational problems, and most importantly develops people and leadership skills that model the way for greater future leadership and advancement of organizational capability and capacity.

Then think and decide which of the ideas will be helpful for you and your people.

Section One

Managing Yourself and Being the Best You Can Be

Leadership is a potent combination of strategy and character.
But if you must do without one, be without strategy.

— Norman Schwarzkopf[*]

1.1 The Story So Far—Your Behavior Matters!

It is now day three into Sam's new role as a change leader.

Sam is acutely aware of the need to be successful as quickly as possible, given the range of business issues the organization wants them to remedy.

Sam decided that it would be pertinent to complete a leadership refresher to ensure that momentum builds early. Specifically, Sam identifies that a focus on building resilience would greatly assist in countering the onslaught of the Volatile, Uncertain, Complex, and Ambiguous (VUCA) world and finds a suitable assessment tool to use.

Sam began the day as usual; got out of bed at 0600, ate breakfast, and then cycled to work. Having arrived, showered, and dressed, Sam was ready for the day ahead at 0730.

---

[*] https://www.brainyquote.com/quotes/norman_schwarzkopf_163145

2 The Business of People: Leadership for the Changing World

Sam has good self-awareness and knew that today could be quite overwhelming. Already there are files piled up on the desk; a very full email inbox; no Sue, Sam's Executive Assistant (on leave); and a To-Do list left by the previous change leader, who left under a cloud. There was a nice welcome card from Pat, the CEO, on behalf of the executive leadership group.

In order to cope, Sam took time to focus, using a technique called ABCD (see Tool S1.1 on page 27) and then thought about what was needed to remain calm and stay present for the tasks at hand.

Sam knows that the best time for their thinking happens in the morning, so scanned and planned in order to prioritize. However, having faced several interruptions from calls and staff, Sam needed to apply emotional intelligence skills to manage the building stress.

Feeling those signs of stress and the ensuing tendency to criticize, and in order to ensure that didn't happen, Sam reminded self about maintaining respect in the workplace. They used an app on their smartphone to check in as to the level of civility being displayed and scored 85 percent. The app feedback came with 10 ideas for improving their respectfulness in the workplace.[*]

As Sam took control, they also remembered that a priority was to develop key internal relationships, especially with Sue. Sam needed to understand what had taken her away on leave. Sam had arranged to meet with the change team, a cross-functional group, at 1130 and invited everyone to meet individually over the next week.

Just before midday Sam received a "good luck" message from a childhood friend who had recently become bankrupt. Sam knew success was not down to luck, but the message gave them food for thought and made Sam consider how it was they got to be in this current role.

Sam was reminded of a few situations in which individual leaders had not managed their personal situations, and this had led them to sabotage themselves, which was preventable had they been able to be more aware.

1.2 Case Study

There are many reasons that people obstruct themselves. One theory of human communication and interaction in the workplace, as detailed in Stewart and Joines's *TA Today*,[†] is a concept called "script," which is described as a life plan, based on the decisions made as a child and reinforced by adults. It is mostly

---

[*] Porath, 2019

[†] Stewart and Joines, 2002

outside of the person's awareness. Reality becomes redefined to "justify" the script—creating a distortion. In order to be the best you can be, we invite you to explore your own script messages by completing an exercise in the Tools section (see Tool S1.2 on page 27).

Here are some examples of how you can get in your own way:

- **Losing your temper.** A leader has a temper and often gets irritated with themselves but takes it out on the team members. The justification is that if the team members gave more notice or time for the work to be done, then the team leader's temper wouldn't be lost!

- **Standing over people.** A leader tends to micromanage people and stands over them to manage the detail of their work. This justification is that as leader they knew more than the worker and did not want them to make a mistake.

- **Not able to make decisions.** A leader is timid and unable to make decisions in ambiguous situations; this leader misses opportunities and fails to get products to the market on time. This leader's justification is that it was important to know all the information prior to deciding and they did not want to lose lots of money, as has happened in the past.

- **Developing an illness.** A leader has developed a terminal illness but is not able to recognize their vulnerability to the situation. They do not have the energy to follow up with things, and the financial situation is becoming untenable. Their justification is that they didn't want to face the distress their death would cause the family.

In each of these situations, the end of the story is this: The outcome of the scenario was that the inability to see the situation for what was there meant a self-fulfilling prophesy occurred and each of the organizations failed.

To avoid the traps that can so easily ensnare a leader, we are sharing with you leadership concepts we have used ourselves and with others—concepts which empower us all to achieve better outcomes.

1.2.1 The Importance of Soft Skills

We know that people who understand and manage their own and others' emotions make superior leaders. These leaders can deal with internal tensions, overcome obstacles, and focus others to work collaboratively. They manage conflict with less fallout and build stronger teams. They are also more balanced in themselves and portray a happier demeanor at work. These leaders understand basic skills of self-awareness and social empathy. They recognize their own feelings and moods and understand their impact on others around them. They are adaptable in today's fast-paced world but predicable in their behavior. They demonstrate emotional intelligence, which is, "The ability to control your own emotions and respond effectively to other's emotions," according to Daniel Goleman,[*] a renowned author on emotional intelligence.

In his 2000 work he states there are key skills that make up an emotionally intelligent person:

- Assertiveness
- Empathy
- Self confidence
- Optimism
- Flexibility
- Self-awareness
- Self-reliance
- Relationship skills

Take some time to reflect. Which of these skills are easy for you to say, hand on heart—I can do this? Which are harder? What would your best friend or life partner say you needed to work on? When you are stressed, which of these skills fly out the window?

The good thing is that you can learn all these competencies. Each of the skills will be covered as you progress through this book.

We have seen projects, programs of work, and businesses fail because leaders lacked the required emotional intelligence and social competence to lead in the modern world.

1.3 Solutions for the Situation

1.3.1 Understanding How Your Brain Works

We understand from neuroscience more now about how the brain works. This body of knowledge is growing continuously. Each area of the brain has certain functions—all aimed at our survival.

---

[*] Goleman, 2000

There are three key concepts to keep in mind that will assist you to be the best that you can be.

a. The brain cannot tell the difference between a social threat and a physical threat.

b. Because we have been programmed to live in groups, our brain's functioning helps us to recognize when our place in the group is threatened.

c. We can continue to learn about anything as long as we have decided we want to. (So, we can change our behavior, our attitudes, our responses to interactions.)

One part of the brain that is crucial to understanding human behavior is the amygdala. "The amygdala is a part of the brain that takes control over what you do even as the thinking brain is deciding what to do," says Daniel Goleman in his blockbuster book, *Emotional Intelligence—Why It Can Matter More Than IQ*.[*] He tells a story about a man from the States who came home to hear noises in his house. Thinking there was a burglar in the house, he grabbed his gun and cautiously headed toward the noises. But what he didn't understand was that his 14-year-old daughter, who had been away, returned home early and, to "surprise" her Dad, hid in a closet and then jumped out on him saying "Boo." This surprised him of course but, in his shock, he was unable to recognize her voice or her face. Tragically, she was shot and died less than a day later.

Knowing how the amygdala part of the brain works and how your thinking affects your feelings is a basic tool in managing yourself. This knowledge will help you to be less stressed, have less conflict, and be more effective and productive.

We are constantly scanning our environment to minimize danger and maximize reward. If we perceive danger, our brain triggers the threat response often known as the "fight or flight" or the "avoid"—and coined the *amygdala hijack,* where we become overwhelmed and are operating out of our prehistoric brain. What we now understand from neuroscience is that we can have the same result from a *perceived* threat—so that, when our core concerns (part of our social identity) get threatened or our values are perceived as being under attack, we can experience a threat response.

Champion of neuro-leadership David Rock[†] identifies five core concerns as part of his SCARF model. These are:

---

[*] Goleman, 2007

[†] Rock, 2009

- **Status** is about relative importance to others. For example, if in a meeting others are introduced and you are not, then this may trigger a threat response.

- **Certainty** relates to being able to predict the future. For example, if you arrive at a meeting and someone has changed the topic without informing you, your threat response is heightened.

- **Autonomy** provides a sense of control over events. For example, when a more senior leader changes an important part of your project without consulting you, you may well find yourself managing a threat response.

- **Relatedness** is a sense of safety with others—a friend rather than a foe. An example of this is entering a room and no one smiles at you.

- **Fairness** is a perception of fair exchanges between people. Here an example is when your colleague gets time to talk about an important aspect of their project for a decent amount of time and you are left with only 30 seconds.

When you have an amygdala hijack, your body reacts to your brain's decision that there is a perceived threat. You might experience your heart pounding, you may sweat or want to go to the bathroom, and your thinking brain will probably go blank.

So, our perception of an event or how we see a social situation may trigger us. This is not being silly or naïve. It is instead our ancient response which, back in the early days of humans, might have meant you starved or in some way could not get access to the resources of the group. This ultimately meant you could not survive. Our ancestors must all have had good ways of recognizing the threat response and working with them, otherwise we would not be here today.

The way the amygdala works and impacts on your thinking is fundamental to developing emotional intelligence.

Now we know that when you experience high emotion, the amygdala can override your logic and cause you to behave in certain ways—to fight, flee, or freeze. Recognizing your emotions can help you to know when you are not functioning at your best.

You will have a clear idea about what works for you. However, here are some techniques that can help you to self-sooth and to calm yourself down in the moment. Some options:

- Breathing

- Singing

- Grounding

- Gratitude

- Focus

- Dancing

- Exercise (puffing)

- Distraction (e.g., thinking about chickens, lunch, or gorse—it doesn't matter what as long as you are not thinking about what distresses you.)

- Rest (which are what morning and afternoon tea and meal breaks are for)

And yes, all of these are possible at work!

We are learning that the current trend among many young people is that they have had little practice with managing threats—social or physical—which means that workplaces are now full of people who need to learn to self-soothe and develop their resilience. This, then, requires leaders who recognize this as a risk for their enterprise and are able to provide the right support and tools for their workers.

So how can you build your ability to manage an increasing number of situations that may trigger your threat response? The first step is to build an awareness of your own personal preferences to thinking, feeling, and working.

1.3.2 Increasing Your Self-Awareness

People can be complicated, but we also follow some basic human behavioral rules.

As a leader, the more you can be consciously aware of the "stories" you are telling yourself—about you, about them, and about what you think they are saying about you—the more you can be aware of your frame of reference and how it is impacting the current interaction. You can explore your thinking in a series of questions and use the insights you get from these reflections.

This concept has been coined the *Identity Conversation*. "This is the conversation we each have with ourselves about what a specific situation means to us"[*] (see Tool S1.3 on page 28).

What we often discover is that the reality we are in is not the reality that others are in.

Madeleine, in her work with people who are in conflict, knows that each time she listens to an affected party, they will have a compelling story to tell, and when she hears the other party, she will hear an equally compelling story.

---

[*] Stone, Patton, and Heen, 1999

8 The Business of People: Leadership for the Changing World

This shows how your frame of reference influences your understanding of what is happening and can affect how you respond.

Following are some techniques to help you build your self-awareness.

Knowing Your Values

In his top-selling book *The Business of Portfolio Management—Boosting Organizational Value,*[*] Iain offers a sample of traits based on leadership principles, styles, and techniques. By adopting—and where necessary, adapting—those, one can certainly demonstrate alignment with the 3P's to Success (Purpose, People, Performance) at a personal level.

These principles, styles, and techniques are shaped and influenced by the personal values we all have. As a leader of people, it is essential that you discover, develop, and enhance your personal values so that a genuine and realistic result emerges. Others then see and experience those, irrespective of whether it is in a social, professional, or personal environment. Underpinning those values are a few "anchors" that give us confidence as well as a high level of consistency in application. Those anchors are *personal purpose, transparency, ethics,* and *professional standards.* Let us explore them a bit further.

- **Personal purpose.** Having a personal purpose is all about being clear on what one wishes to achieve in a variety of settings—for example, at home, at work, or on the sports field. The personal purpose should be a multiple-year vision so that it goes beyond a short-term trend that can get swayed by indulgence or stimulus.

- **Transparency.** Transparency is about being comfortable sharing and showing one's weaknesses with others. It is also about being truthful towards yourself as well as others. Being clear, open, candid, and, where possible, simple are the keys to success. Remember that in the VUCA world there is no place for leaders who "hold cards close to their chest" and do not disclose or share relevant information. Agility or nimbleness is the key to harvesting opportunities, and transparency will greatly assist in fast decision making by encouraging collaboration amongst colleagues and team members.

- **Ethics.** Related to ones' personal purpose and transparency is the notion of ethics as a part of one's "values DNA." Generally, ethics are related to a code of conduct that exists within a profession, such as medical, project management, and engineering. Most professions have a comprehensive

---

[*] Fraser, 2017

set of ethics that govern the professional behavior when operating within that profession. Codes of conduct that govern ethical behavior can be simple or complex, threatening or non-threatening, local or global, statute or principle based.

To assist you, we have an Exploring Your Values Exercise in the Tools section for you to complete (see Tool S1.7 on page 34).

Example: Some years ago, Iain had the honor to sponsor the development and release of the Project Management Institute's (PMI®) Code of Ethics and Professional Conduct,* first released in 2006. This guide was, and still is, based on four core attributes that drive ethical conduct for the project management profession. The attributes are *honesty, responsibility, respect,* and *fairness*—a simple yet powerful grouping that can and should be applied to all aspects of ones' life, irrespective of belonging to PMI or not.

- **Professional standards.** To complete the anchors, we turn our attention to professional standards. In the context of values, we need to channel our focus on professional standards which guide what we do and when and where we do it. By being professional, we perform our duties within certain parameters that are set by our personal purpose, our ethical behavior, and standards that are relevant. Those standards can be a combination of regulation, governance, and professional conduct, all of which present a set of somewhat flexible parameters.

Each of us, as well as Sam, must make sure that we know our values, clarify them, and apply them at every opportunity. This underpins the adoption and use of principles and leadership styles, together with your thinking styles and techniques. Demonstrating your values in a consistent and genuine manner will have people keen to be associated with you and follow you.

Recognizing Feelings

Feelings are created by what you think, and they provide important data for problem solving. Ignoring your feelings will hinder your problem-solving ability. Because feelings provide you with information, recognizing what the feeling is and what has triggered it can help you to decide whether to minimize it or pay attention to it. (See Tool S1.4 on page 29 to help you unearth your true feelings about a situation.) You may find it helpful to complete the worksheet for each triggered situation. That way you are building a data set of

---

* PMI, 2006

your responses, and this information will assist you to take account of what is happening to you.

However, it is useful to also know that just because you have a feeling does not mean that the story you are telling yourself is currently valid or the truth of the situation. It does, however, explain your response.

For example, if you already know that you feel fearful when speaking at a meeting, and this is an old habit, you can dial back your fear. However, if you are in a meeting and you begin to feel ignored, you might want to examine where that has come from. If your feeling comes from an old habit (which is not useful in the here and now), then do some work so that old feeling habit does not contaminate the present. However, if the feeling is based on the dynamics in the room, then you are safer to address the here-and-now situation.

Knowing how your brain works and what your personal triggers are will assist you to be mindful in any given situation. Being able to recognize when you get stuck and knowing strategies that work for you in that moment can free you from old, unhelpful patterns.

Continue to practice and maintain a positive attitude. There are many strategies for keeping calm in the present:

- Name the feeling.

- Ask yourself a question—for example, what did you have for breakfast? What color is your underwear?

- Notice your body stance.

- Breathe slowly.

- Use grounding techniques—notice your feet, notice objects in the room, notice the sounds around you.

However, it may be that you need to reflect on your overall stress level, so check these things:

- Get the right amount of sleep.

- Eat healthily.

- Exercise well.

- Set limits.

- Give yourself affirmations.

- Visualize.

- Laugh.

- Pray.

- Spend time with friends and family.

- Be assertive.

- Be kind to yourself.

Recognize Your Thinking Style Preferences

Today a great deal of emphasis is put on the assessment of people using personality systems. The range of systems is staggering—from the very straightforward, in which assessments are mocked up and done around the Saturday afternoon barbeque table, to highly advanced and expensive systems that seemingly require a masters' degree in psychology to operate and decypher!

In the VUCA world, more emphasis needs to be put on understanding and use of thinking-style preferences. By understanding how we as individuals prefer to think and how others prefer to think, we can make huge strides toward developing high-performing individuals. Subsequently, this leads to high-performing teams that unite and quickly and efficiently solve challenges of all types.

The work done by the Herrmann International Group via its Whole Brain® Thinking Model* is a leading source of the science and research into thinking style preferences. The Herrmann International Group work presents a color-coded quadrant perspective that relates four thinking style preferences to different areas of the brain—that is, left and right, plus top (cerebral) and bottom (limbic). How we think has a considerable impact on how we are perceived by others and what relationship develops as a consequence. More on this in subsequent sections.

Understand Learning States

Understanding the way in which we learn, process information, and interact with the world and its information is a critical awareness needed by all leaders. Knowing your learning state preferences and biases will assist you in your negotiations, when under pressure, and when working with people with difficult behaviors.

All of us have these, but we use them in different ways. These states are *conscious, subconscious,* and *unconscious.* In some ways they can be attributed to the logical versus the creative parts of the brain.

---

* Herrmann International Group, n.d.

12　The Business of People: Leadership for the Changing World

- **Conscious.** The Conscious learning state is dominated by the left part of our brain, which in turn is structured and rule-bound—for example, by school, by military, by law. This is our default learning state, which in many ways determines our personality type.

- **Subconscious.** The Subconscious learning state is triggered by the conscious part of our minds. It is often thought of as the "uh-huh" part of our brains, in that once triggered, we gain clear resolution on a problem, task, or other endeavor. Think of it as a giant database of information that we have stored since our very youngest years. The recall often happens when our conscious minds are resting or not fully engaged on a specific topic. All of us have experienced uh-huh moments during which a solution suddenly enters our minds, seemingly from nowhere. An example is when a solution to a work problem suddenly enters our minds while driving home, or while relaxing in front of the television. Another example is when the uh-huh moment wakes us up during the middle of the night with an idea or answer.

- **Unconscious.** Unconscious learning is the unstructured learning state that is free of logic and generally unhindered by our stored conscious and subconscious states. This state allows us to develop our learning by breaking the rules of habit, boundary, or stimulus. This creative learning state assists us in coming up with novel ways of doing things.

In a leadership context, having a deeper understanding of the three learning states and how they can be developed will enhance your capability as a leader of people.

Your Learning Styles

Supplementing the learning *states* are learning *styles*. The classification of auditory, kinesthetic, visual, vocal, and spatial are well known. Perhaps less well known is that we are able to use combinations of learning styles, in order of preference, to allow us to learn in different ways. Our number one preference is our favorite, while our number five preference is rarely used. An example of this is that people with preferences for kinesthetic learning will often enjoy visual stimulus as a second style (see Tool S1.5 on page 30 to clarify your own learning styles).

Recognizing Your Working Style

How you think impacts your behavior and your working style, and again we encourage you to explore your own behavioral strategies, especially when things

Managing Yourself and Being the Best You Can Be   13

get a little stressed. These are not right or wrong, they are the way you tick. The working style model was developed by Julie Hay* and based on original work by Taibi Kahler.† We have combined this with Keith Tudor's "Take it" style‡ to include the overindulged personality. See if you can spot your preferred working style (see Tool S1.6 on page 32). You may even be able to recognize yourself from the name of each style: Be Perfect, Please People, Hurry Up, Try Hard, Be Strong, and Go for It.

Knowing When You Are Vulnerable

While you may know how you operate in any given situation, you also need to recognize your personal vulnerabilities and, more importantly, when you are beginning to feel vulnerable. That way you can act sooner to counteract the situation.

As a mother of a three-month-old baby, Madeleine was really scared when she noticed a bleeding mole, as she knew what it meant. She took herself straight away to a doctor, but he said not to worry; she went to her own GP, who also said not to worry. Three doctors later, they had all said "not to worry." Eventually, and still concerned, she insisted that her doctor remove the mole for biopsy. Post operation analysis discovered that it was an unusual form of a level four cancer. Had it been left on her body, she surely would have died.

In 2006 a young Japanese man was in the Tokyo subway when terrorists launched a deadly gas attack. He rang his father to find out what he should do. The father didn't answer, and the few minutes the young man waited meant that he was unable to escape the life-threatening situation. He had not grown up enough to make his own risk assessment in the moment.

Most situations in which leaders find themselves in today's workplaces are not life threatening. However, the reality is that sometimes we are faced with life-threatening situations, and we need to know how to respond immediately. Regardless of the threat, being able to recognize your vulnerability and name the feeling means that you can find the correct solution for the situation and then act to that end. Awareness of your vulnerability allows you to notice suffering or potential suffering and to accept the reality you face—with no judgment. Being aware means that you acknowledge the true nature of the situation, which in turn leads you to be able to problem solve.

Being aware of your vulnerabilities will assist you to not fall into a repetitive pattern of self-sabotage. In fact, recognizing your vulnerability gives you power

---

* Hay, 2009
† Kahler and Tahibi, 2009
‡ Tudor, 2008

over your circumstances. Being vulnerable is not the same as being helpless. Being vulnerable provides you with a level of power that, if ignored, would make you powerless.

How to recognize when you are vulnerable: First observe your body, then your feelings, then the awareness of what you are saying to yourself. If you have been the type who doesn't allow yourself to recognize trouble, then this process may take time. Remember, your brain is trying to protect you from your old threat. Time has changed your circumstances. That threat does not exist in your current world. You can learn new ways.

Example: A 47-year-old worker was sent an email letting him know that his workplace had selected him to receive a $30,000 university scholarship. This worker said to himself that this could not possibly be for him, and so he deleted the email. Luckily for him, his boss asked what he had done about it and encouraged him to take the opportunity. And he did.

Establishing Clear Boundaries

Previously in this section, we discussed being clear about your values. However, having clarity is not enough. Once you have decided on the values that you want to uphold in your life, then you need to go about living them. Being able to set limits and live your values will be what sets you apart as a great leader.

What we know is that when your boundary hits up against someone else's boundary—as it is sure to do—then you need to have some techniques up your sleeve to manage the situation.

The first of these is to be clear when you have come to a boundary. You will know this if you consider what Sarri Gilman has described as the "Compass in your Tummy."* The compass says *yes* or *no* when a tricky situation comes up. *Yes,* you feel you can go with the situation, or *no*—this is not right. The tricky part is when two or more of your values coincide. Being clear about the ranking of your values can help you to decide. If you go with your *no* and communicate that, you may create some conflict in the short term, but you will have been consistent with your values and beliefs. Frequently, the conflict is short lived, but transgressing a value boundary will be with you forever. It becomes the slippery slope of being pushed and pulled by others—not a good trait for a leader.

Sometimes leaders have trouble saying no. We offer some possible words that might get you started. Check out Tool S1.8—Many Ways to Say No—on page 36. Knowing your preferences in these areas will build your self-awareness and assist you in your leadership function.

---

* Gilman, 2005

1.3.3 How Can You Change to Be the Best You Can Be?

It is all very well to know who we are and how we tick, but what happens if you discover that you have behaviors or thought patterns that are making it difficult for you to lead.

Read on, and you will discover some handy tips about personal change.

The Role of Habits

A bad habit can kill you. Glen Singleman and Heather Swan,[*] an Australian couple, gave a talk about learning to wing-suit base-jump, which went terribly wrong. They were in Italy on a cliff 4,500 feet high. When Glen first tried the jump, he forgot he was in a wing jump suit, and his body reacted as if he was in a parachute. He had arched his back like a usual base jump; however, because he was in a wing suit, the suit caused him to be the wrong way round and upside down—falling at breakneck speed straight towards the ground. His head was centimeters from the cliff, and he had nowhere to fly, because the cliff was in his face. Glen knew he had to change his position in order to flip over and fly out to a safe landing—all the while free falling to certain death. He knew that he had to manage his mind in order to correct his potentially fatal mistake. Clearly, he did this, because he survived to tell us the tale. Knowing what he did about how the brain worked, he was able to recognize the situation he was in and work out how he needed to adapt.

Knowing that you can change old habits can free you to change those things that get in the way of being the leader you want to be.

Madeleine passed a woman as she was walking a while ago and stopped to talk. The woman was smoking a cigarette. The woman said, "I know I shouldn't be doing this . . ." Madeleine said, I can help you with that if you want to change. Long story short, the woman had made a decision to keep smoking. Madeleine said, "Well don't feel bad, live with your decision. That is ok. When you change your mind, you will make a decision to stop and change will happen." The woman smiled and said, "Yes." This short tale reminds us that we cannot change without a prior decision to do so.

According to Charles Duhigg in his book *The Power of Habit*,[†] the definition of a habit is: "A set of behaviors that are repeated regularly and tend to occur unconsciously." The human brain creates habits in order to be efficient. Habits can be changed and replaced anytime we choose. There are three parts to a habit—a *cue*, a *routine*, and a *reward*. Sometimes it takes a little work to uncover

---

[*] Singleman and Swan, 2003

[†] Duhigg, 2012

16 The Business of People: Leadership for the Changing World

what the real cue is. Carefully observe the following five things that scientists say might cue the habit: *location, time, emotional state, other people,* and *what happened just before.* Keep noticing.

How to Change a Habit

Kennedy, a senior executive, was being coached because she had a habit of yelling at her staff when she was under stress. Prior to the coaching, the outcome for Kennedy and her direct reports was less than positive. Kennedy recognized that this was something she wanted to change. She became aware of the cue which set off the bad habit routine. Once she understood her thinking and knew there was hope that she could change, she was able to do just that. Sometime later she sat an assessment center psychological test for a new job, and her CEO was amazed when the tester said that she had a changed personality!! The truth is we can change our habits.

You have the power to change any habit or behavior you choose, even very old habits. The key is to learn what the cue is and what the new rewards are and change the routine.

In addition, Alan Deutschman, in his book *Change or Die,*[*] suggests that there are three ideas to focus on when you want to change a habit:

- **Relate**—a deep belief that a change is possible; real hope for a different future.

- **Repeat**—practice and practice: develop the new habit, a new way of doing things.

- **Reframe**—new ways of thinking about the new habit.

The really interesting thing about the formation of habits is that they form in the same way for individuals, organizations, and communities. This is compelling information for great leaders.

Sometimes we are not sure if we want to change; see Figure 1.1. Do you want to change a habit? Answer these questions to explore the habit you want to change:

1. What are the good things about the old habit?

2. What would happen if you didn't change? Now, in one year, in five years?

3. Who wants you to change the habit, and what are their concerns?

---

[*] Deutschman, 2007

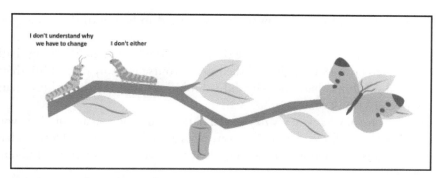

Figure 1.1 Grubs to Butterflies

4. What tells you that you cannot make the change?

5. What habits have you been able to change in the past? Think of as many as you can.

6. Do you really want to make a change? If yes, keep going. If not, allow yourself not to change and accept the consequences of your choice.

7. Who can help you to think this through further?

Managing Destructive Thinking

As we have said before, our feelings are determined by the thoughts we are having about a situation. For example, an employee was asked to go and talk with her manager, whose office was in another part of the city. All the way to the manager's office, the employee was thinking, "What have I done wrong, maybe I am in big trouble, maybe they will fire me, maybe the manager is really cross with me . . ." She felt more and more worried, anxious, and fearful. Then as she got closer to the office, she remembered that the manager had worked with her for five years, had never been mean or rude, and had always thought she had done a good job. She began to feel more relaxed and peaceful about the meeting.

The way you think about a situation can change your feelings toward it. Taking time to recognize what you are saying to yourself allows a reflection of that awareness and enables you to decide how you want to think in the here and now. Being aware of what you are thinking and the meaning you are giving to a situation is an important skill for managing yourself.

Our feelings come from our thoughts. Our assumptions come from the thoughts we have that we are unaware of having. Our assumptions are rooted deep in our view of the world, our frame of reference.

18   The Business of People: Leadership for the Changing World

In order to build your self-awareness, you need to be mindful of what you are thinking.

How can you notice what you are thinking and why you are thinking that? One way is to notice a thought and then to ask yourself, "Why did I think that? and why did I think that? and why did I think that? and why did I think that? and why did I think that?"

Being aware of what you say to yourself daily about who you are and how you unconsciously reinforce messages to yourself is a useful awareness. Notice what these thoughts are saying and then decide if you need say something different to yourself.

An example of someone not managing destructive thinking happened in 2014, when a New Zealand man was so overwhelmed by his circumstances and so angry with his perceived lack of government support that he got up one morning, walked into the social service office, and shot two of the workers. Clearly an extreme case of emotional distress and a consequent action which did not solve the problem at all. In fact, his actions made his circumstances infinitely worse and caused untold suffering for others.

Being aware of your emotions and destructive thinking can help you to recognize when you are not functioning at your best. What do you already do to monitor your feelings and those background thoughts? What can you do to keep yourself on an even keel? What can you do to stop yourself tipping over the edge?

Remember how you learn best and think of what you can do to practice and enhance your emotional intelligence skills.

Recognizing When You Are Stuck

Sometimes when we are overwhelmed or upset by a situation, we get stuck. When this happens, we cannot see that we are stuck. So, the initial thing to do is to recognize that you are stuck.

According to Stewart and Joines in their internationally recognized book on TA,[*] there are four things that we habitually do when we get stuck and unable to problem solve. We:

1. Do nothing. For example, sitting at a restaurant, thirsty, and complaining about not having water delivered and not recognizing that you can walk to the water dispenser and get the water yourself.

2. Perfect things to make them look good but without solving the problem. For example, avoiding solving the real problem by making something else look really great.

---

[*] Stewart and Joines, 2002

Managing Yourself and Being the Best You Can Be   19

3. Agitate (this is Madeleine's personal favorite). For example, thinking that she had lost her passport, she kept looking and looking and couldn't hear the instruction to look in another bag.

4. We become incapacitated or numb ourselves (suffer from migraines, get sick, drunk, drugged). For example, as a student when faced with going to a work placement where the children were treated cruelly, Madeleine discovered that every Wednesday morning, she was too unwell to get to the placement.

These are all forms of self-sabotage. Which is your personal favorite? Think about the last time you had a tricky situation. What did you do?

So, what is happening? We cannot see the issue for what it is. Others may well be able to see what we are unable to. The concept is called discounting, and it is an unconscious process and a form of denial. It is an internal mechanism that occurs outside of our awareness and involves minimizing or ignoring some aspect of ourselves, others, and/or the situation. We discount in order to maintain and reinforce our frame of reference, our view of the world. In order to understand more about what we can't see, we can take time to explore how we do see the situation.

There are four levels of discounting:

1. Discounting the *existence* of the problem

2. Discounting the *significance* of the problem

3. Discounting the *change possibility* of the problem

4. Discounting our *personal ability* to solve the problem

Julie Hay and Anne Tucker developed the Steps to Success tool,[*] which guides you to develop questions to help you become more aware.

Julie, in her book *Transactional Analysis for Trainers,*[†] developed specific questions for each level.

- **Level 1: Existence**

    o What is happening?

    o Who is saying and doing what?

    o What expressions, gestures, body movements are there?

---

[*] Hay and Tucker, 2010

[†] Hay, 2009

20   The Business of People: Leadership for the Changing World

- **Level 2: Significance**
  - o What might the situational evidence mean?
  - o If there is an issue or problem, what might it be?
  - o How is any of this significant?
- **Level 3: Change possibilities**
  - o What solutions are available (even small steps that might create some movement)?
  - o What options might lead to better outcomes?
  - o What options might lead to worse outcomes?
- **Level 4: Skills**
  - o What skills do you need to implement various solutions?
  - o What relevant skills do you have already (including those you've previously used only in different circumstances)?
  - o How can you acquire any additional skills needed?
- **Level 5: Strategies**
  - o How will you plan to implement solutions?
  - o What help or support might you get from others?
  - o How might others get in your way—and what will you do about that?
- **Level 6: Success**
  - o What is your rationale for not acting?
  - o What are the benefits from not acting?
  - o What are you afraid may happen when you act—and how will you deal with that?

1.3.4 *Your Current Work Situation—An Awareness of the Pool in Which You Are Swimming*

Volatility, Uncertainty, Complexity, and Ambiguity

Earlier we touched on the unclear nature of the modern world and how that, together with other elements of the VUCA world, suggests that our leadership and people management capabilities need adaption. Ambiguity creates uncertainty, and it is uncertainty that is the greatest cause of reluctance to change. Habits revolve around a certain environment and get exposed and threatened when change is introduced. When there is doubt, uneasiness usually follows.

For example, a leader who is exposed to ambiguous information that is to be used for decision making is likely to stall the decision and potentially miss an opportunity. Ambiguity is not about each of us scoring on an optimistic/pessimistic scale; it is about relying on leadership courage, which includes assessing the ambiguous situation as best one can, setting a direction that seeks to protect or gain some form of value, yet at the same time knowing that the direction may not prove sufficient, thereby forcing a change. Dealing with ambiguity is about setting a leadership example which embraces a high degree of flexibility—agility, if you prefer—and encouraging others to follow.

The vague, unclear, hazy nature of ambiguity means that high levels of certainty, which were so sought after in the 20th century to minimize risk, are likely not to exist in the VUCA world, in which speed and nimbleness are the key attributes for success.

As a leader, you will need to be comfortable with ambiguity and develop strategies to assist your decision making. Being clear about your values, ethics, and boundaries will help you develop direction in uncertain times. These will become the moments that define you as a leader. If you play the long game, knowing your purpose and attitudes, you will create your leadership brand, and others will see your value. This will encourage trust in a dynamic world. Ways of helping with this are:

- Being clear about your values and those of your organization

- Having clear boundaries

- Having problem-solving strategies

- Knowing yourself and your vulnerabilities and those which get you stuck

The Need for Resilience and Optimism

The changing nature of the VUCA-impacted world is challenging leaders in ways not previously experienced or obvious. Being able to manage yourself and lead others through challenging times is a key skill of great leaders. In addition, recent information highlights the increasing risk to businesses in which employees are managing higher levels of mental fragility, which is another sign of the times.

The personal attribute of resilience is getting more attention because it is being seen as a skill differentiator. It seems that the challenges presented by the VUCA world require us to be tough within ourselves, to be springy in our approaches, and to have a strong and robust spirit. These skills need to be applied not in a foolhardy manner but in more of a heroic manner. Examples include making the decision when others cannot or will not, trying again after experiencing a large failure, and changing direction when no one else wishes to or knows how to.

Resilience is a deep-rooted personal attribute that often is shaped by our past life experiences. It gives us drive that is supported with a healthy dose of optimism and anticipation. It also allows us to be assertive in our leadership roles, knowing that if we initially fail, we can bounce back quickly. It is important that resilience is not a single thing, but more that it is made up of a collection of personal attributes that might include focus, drive, optimism, and assertiveness. As mentioned earlier, our past life experiences will have a significant influence, as do our most basic flight or fight reaction choices.

Iain had a series of traumatic experiences as a young child that were to shape his future. Rather than trying to hide from the trauma, he chose to fight, not in a physical manner, but rather in a driven manner. Examples of success achieved throughout his life include sporting successes, career successes, and success in his hobbies, family, and relationships. Today he admits to still having a desire to do better in everything he does—a deep-down drive instilled from those early experiences.

As Sam embarks on their leadership journey, they will experience success and failure. However, it is how they develop resilience that will determine how they manage themselves and how this impacts on people around them and reporting to them.

If you want to build your resilience there are active steps that you can take:

1. Take care of yourself

2. Connect with others

3. Take advantage of your strengths

4. Be active

5. Use and develop your key skills

6. Use your sense of humor

7. Keep a positive outlook

8. Keep learning

9. Stay tuned in

10. Do things for others without expecting a return

Another personal attribute is optimism. Being optimistic can change your life. Optimism is often defined as a disposition to expect the best and view events and situations in a positive light. Knowing that, we see that optimism gives people a sense of real hope and energy to keep trying that allows time for a potential solution to arise. The elements of optimism are hopefulness, anticipation, and a sense of a compelling future.

Research about the benefits of being optimistic shows that optimists tend to:

- Have better physical health
- Enjoy greater success at school, work, and sport
- Be in more satisfying relationships
- Have better mental health, reporting less depression and anxiety
- Live longer than pessimists

Interestingly, as you can change your habits, you can develop increased capacity to be optimistic. In most circumstances, optimism is beneficial but does need to be tempered. People who are excessively optimistic may not have realistic expectations about the possibility of bad things occurring, and so are caught unprepared when they do. They may also fail to take responsibility for the impact of their own behavior, resulting in relationship difficulties.

To explain how optimism develops, the following research demonstrates [as a note, these experiments would not be allowed today]. In the 1950s, Dr. Curt Paul Richter carried out a series of experiments that tested how long rats could swim in a high-sided bucket of circulating water before drowning. Dr. Richter found that, under normal conditions, a lab rat could swim for an average of 15 minutes before giving up and sinking. However, if he took the rats out just before drowning, dried them off and let them rest briefly, then put them back into the same buckets of water, the rats would swim an average of 60 hours before giving up and drowning. If a rat was saved, dried off and given a brief rest before going back into the bucket, it would survive 240 times longer than if it was not.

Dr. Richter's conclusion was that the rats were able to swim longer because they were given hope. That is, the rats were able to keep going longer because they were able to predict they might be saved again, and that gave them hope, which in turn gave them energy to keep going. The rats had a clear picture of what being saved looked like, so they kept swimming for it.

Having and Maintaining Focus

Focus is important in leadership and business generally. It is the process of being able to attune your mind to the task at hand and remove all other disruptions and clutter from your thinking. When we are focused, time disappears and work gets done. When we are unfocused or distracted, then time can drag and work becomes a drudge.

Focus has been termed *the gateway of all thinking*. Put simply, if you cannot focus, you cannot think well or make decisions. This leads to inefficiency and poor work outputs.

It appears that the human attention span is diminishing because of digital connectedness and the search for novelty; our brains are becoming addicted to the constancy of the "endorphin hit." However, as always, there is hope. Elie Vensesky and Patrycja Slawuta, co-authors of *Hack Your Brain*,[*] say that focus is like a muscle, and you can grow your ability to focus. Here is how:

1. Decide that you want to increase your focus time

2. Calm yourself before starting a task

3. Identify what you need to focus on—for the year, month, week, day, hour, and now

4. Silence the email/put away your devices

5. Take time for short breaks

6. Rehydrate yourself

7. Make sure you are working in the right temperature for you—too hot, too cold, and you will lose focus

8. Play music that you like

Assertiveness

As a young boy, Madeleine's father was asked by a gruff, rotund family friend if he would like a pocket knife. Her father was excited to be offered such a wonderful gift; however, he felt it was an extravagance, so in order to be polite, her father said, "Oh, that is very kind," in a coy fashion, "but I couldn't . . . ," all the while hoping the man would insist. However, the family friend put the pocket knife away in his own pocket. He then leaned towards her father and whispered in his ear, "Let that be a lesson to you. If you want something that is offered to you, take it and be thankful."

Being able to ask for what you want and stand up for yourself is a key skill in becoming more potent in the world.

---

[*] Venezky and Slawuta, 2014

Managing Yourself and Being the Best You Can Be   25

So, what actually is being assertive? We could refer to it as "standing up for yourself in such a way that ensures that the rights of others are not transgressed."

Using an assertive communication style means that your opinions, feelings, and wants are clearly stated without violating the rights of others. The underlying message is: "You and I may have our differences, but we are equally entitled to express ourselves to one another."

Sometimes we are not sure when we should speak up. Figure 1.2 shows a flow diagram that can assist you to reflect on what might stop you from speaking out when you need to or know you should.

However, even if we want to or know we should speak up, we may not be sure of the words to use. For an assertiveness template that will help you to build your words, see Tool S1.9 on page 36.

Personal Courage is a combination of factors that collectively drive action: factors such as believing in yourself and building your potential, doing what you want and trusting yourself to make the right decision, sitting in the driver's seat and taking control of your life, making your own decisions and being honest with yourself and others, accepting changes and flowing with them, dealing with your problems and asking others for help, offering your opinions and communicating your fears and doubts, accepting abundance and allowing yourself to succeed. Courage is about trying again and doing new things and loving yourself and others unconditionally, even when you do not know all the permutations of a given situation.

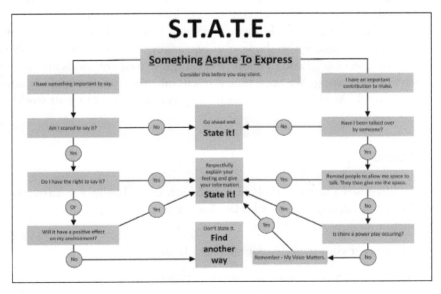

Figure 1.2   STATE Tool

You practice being courageous when you feel afraid, name the fear, let it go then do what you really want to do. You practice courage when you admit mistakes, learn from them, and ask for help when you need it. You can do this by recognizing your unconscious self-talk and understanding where the fear comes from. Is it a current situation or is it an old story you have been carrying around with you? Next recognize who and what gives you strength and find ways to draw on that, even when the chips are down. Take the time to plan for the worst-case scenario and keep on practicing.

Understanding the need for personal courage is about stepping forward even when you are unsure. It's a form of trusting your gut yet balancing with your head and heart. You will know that you are being successful in being courageous when you do what is right for you even when it is hard and scary. You will notice that you can find strength in your heart even when you are afraid, and you will also notice you are willing to try new things.

1.4 Case Study

Positive outcome example: As a young man, Iain completed a psychometric assessment for an employer in Scotland, which at that time assessed his skills and abilities and specifically sought leadership capability. Some 15 years later in New Zealand, he was tested again by another employer and discovered that his assessment results had changed, albeit there remained core traits of leadership capability.

As you learn and grow, your brain develops new habits and your ways of being change. Your experiences also shape your personality. Knowing that growth is possible, you can change and develop. You can grow your soft skills and create new ways of interacting. We hope that you will take the initiative and consider what you would like to develop and then apply your new ways to your world.

1.5 Tools

We have identified a range of tools that we have used and believe can assist you to perform consistently well as a leader. You may use and adapt these tools to apply in a number of ways:

- To support your own development as a leader

- To share with your colleagues and team members

- To support your wider family and friends

As a basis for developing other tools that might suit you more

As a resource for developing and encouraging other leaders

In most cases each tool can be scaled up to use individually, with members of a group/team or across the whole organization.

Tool S1.1: Focus Exercise

ABCD for Focus: Close your eyes and have someone else read this out or record it and play back to yourself.

a. **Anatomy.** Check in with your body, legs, arms, face, feet, hands. Notice areas of tension and relax.

b. **Breathe deeply.** Right down to your stomach, slow breaths for one minute.

c. **Connection.** To the floor, to the earth and to the planet. Check your body position in your seat or as you stand.

d. **Distraction.** Notice the noise outside the room or space you are in, notice the distraction in your mind of other matters. Bring your attention back to the here and now and to the matter at hand.

You are now ready to focus on what you have chosen.

Tool S1.2: Script Exercises

First, read through the exercises, and before doing either, ask yourself: Do you want to do it? Listen carefully to your compass. If you choose no, then don't. If you choose yes, then ask this question of yourself: Do you want to do this exercise on your own or do you want someone to be there for you during or after? Listen to yourself. Take care of yourself.

So, you have decided to continue. Following are two exercises. Decide which one you want to use.

1. Look around you and choose an object. Stick with the first object you choose. Imagine you are that object, be that object. What does it do? How is it treated? What value does it have? What does this mean for you? Sit back and reflect. Notice your feelings—sometimes they are strong. Take care of you. Notice your thinking. Ask what this means for you now.

2. Think of your favorite childhood story, movie, play, family history, tale. Now think about the characters in that story. Who do you most closely identify with? What is it you identify with? How does the story begin, what happens in the middle, and how does it end? How has that character played out in your life? Now sit back and reflect. Notice your feelings—sometimes they are strong. Take care of you. Notice your thinking. Ask what this means for you now.

Tool S1.3: Identity Conversation

Think about a difficult leadership situation. Remember it well. Then answer the following questions.

Question 1: What made it hard for you?

Question 2: What did you tell yourself about what was happening? What "names" were you calling them or yourself?

Question 3: What did you tell yourself the other person was thinking about you?

Question 4: Who have you observed that is able to manage situations like this in a way that you admire?

Question 5: What do they do that impresses you?

Question 6: What are some ways that will help you to manage a difficult leadership situation differently in the future?

Tool S1.4: Identifying Feelings Worksheet

Situation Example	My Thoughts	How My Body Responded	What Feelings I Had	My Interpretation of What Data My Feelings Are Giving Me	Action I Need to Take
I had a disagreement with a customer	Oh, I can't be bothered with this today	Flustered, red face, and heart racing	Irritation	There are other things going on with my family and I don't want to have to deal with other things	Options: Write my thoughts, talk to a friend. I plan to go to supervisor with my journaling

30   The Business of People: Leadership for the Changing World

Tool S1.5: Learning Style Preferences

Tool	Item	Tick Your Preference
Neuro-linguistic accessing—using auditory, visual, kinesthetic, and spatial cues	Auditory: ". . . it sounds like . . ." "Does that ring true?"	
	Visual: ". . . it looks like . . ." "Does that look good?"	
	Kinesthetic: ". . . it feels like . . ." "Does that run smoothly to you?"	
	Spatial: "I would like to take it apart and see how it works."	
Deductive (big picture) and Inductive (little pieces) thinking preferences	Deductive: "I need to see the big picture." "How does this fit in?"	
	Inductive: "What steps will we need to take?" "What makes this work?"	
Introvert and extravert characteristics	Introvert: Needs time to think between activities in order to process information. Gets energy from being quiet and away from others.	
	Extravert likes to talk with others to process information. Gets energy from engaging with others.	

Tool S1.5: Learning Style Preferences (cont.)

Tool	Item	Tick Your Preference
Direct or indirect learning	Direct learning is where the "teacher" provides experiences so the learner can see the direct link. Where there are set goals, with outcomes described, and so you know if you have learned "it" or not.	
	Indirect learning is where the learner is working through an activity and they learn what they need to know through their experience.	
Growth or fixed mindset; Carol Dweck and colleagues[a]	Growth mindset is a belief that you can learn and change.	
	Fixed mindset means you will accept how things are without believing you can influence the outcome.	
Optimistic or pessimistic	Optimistic—see the potential and starts you. Pessimistic—see the problem and stops you.	

[a] Dweck et al., n.d.

Tool S1.6: Working Styles

Style	Strengths	Pitfalls	Taking Advantage of This Style
Be perfect	Is accurate, checks carefully Well organized, looks ahead for potential problems	Includes too much detail, checks over and over Criticizes over minor details, rarely satisfied	Set realistic standards of performance and accuracy. Practice asking yourself what the consequences really are. Make a point of telling others that their mistakes are not serious.
Please People	Good team member, encourages harmony Intuitive and aware, considers others	Anxious for approval of others, will not confront Feels misunderstood, hurt by criticism	Start asking questions to check what people want instead of guessing. Please yourself more often and ask people for what you want. Practice telling other people clearly when you have a differing opinion.
Hurry up	Works quickly, responds well to deadlines Gets a lot done in a short time	Makes mistakes, lacks attention to detail Gets impatient, finishes others' sentences	Plan your work in stages, setting interim time frames. Concentrate on listening to others until they finish speaking. Learn relaxation techniques and use them regularly.

Style	Strengths	Pitfalls	Taking Advantage of This Style
Try Hard	Enthusiastic, energetic, with new ideas Thorough at following up all possibilities	Loses interest and moves on to new things Tends not to finish, others have to take over	Stop offering to do all the extra jobs. Make a plan that includes finishing a task and then stick to the plan through to the conclusion. Check out what is expected and complete that.
Be strong	Calm under pressure, copes with stress Conscientious, strong sense of duty	Will not ask for help or admit weakness May seem cold and distant or overly jovial	Keep a task and a time log to monitor your workload. Ask others to help you. Take up a spare-time activity that you really enjoy.
Go for it	Uses resources enthusiastically Is certain with no doubt "Go getter"	Over-consumption Likes to get "one over" Can be abrupt	Recognize the true cost to self and others. Reflect on how much is enough. Explore sustainable options.

Tool S1.7: Exploring Your Values

What do you want most out of life? There are 24 values listed below. Mark the column to the right of each value statement that best represents you.

	Values	Extremely Important	Important	Not Important
1.	**Responsibility**. Being accountable for actions relating to people or results.			
2.	**Wealth**. Having many possessions and plenty of money for the things one wants.			
3.	**Trustworthiness**. Being honest, straightforward, and frank.			
4.	**Skill**. Being able to use knowledge effectively; being good at doing something important to you and others.			
5.	**Spirituality**. An inner sense of something greater that self.			
6.	**Recognition**. Being important, well-liked, and accepted.			
7.	**Power**. Possession of control, authority, or influence over others.			
8.	**Pleasure**. Satisfaction, gratification, fun, joy.			
9.	**Physical Appearance**. Concern for being attractive; being neat, clean, and well groomed.			
10.	**Morality**. Believing in and keeping ethical standards, personal honour, and integrity.			
11.	**Loyalty**. Maintaining allegiance to a person, group, or institution.			
12.	**Love**. Warmth, caring, going out of your way to support.			
13.	**Knowledge**. Seeking truth, information, or principles for satisfaction or curiosity.			

Values	Extremely Important	Important	Not Important
14. **Achievement**. Accomplishments: results brought about by resolve, persistence, or endeavor.			
15. **Justice**. Treating others fairly or impartially; conforming to truth, fact, or reason.			
16. **Honesty**. Being frank and genuine with everyone.			
17. **Health**. Sound body and eating, sleeping, and exercising enough.			
18. **Creativity**. The creation of new ideas and designs; being innovative.			
19. **Work**. One's lifetime effort.			
20. **Family**. One's present and future family.			
21. **Education**. School, college, vocational training, life-time learning.			
22. **Kindness**. Gentle, considerate, helpful, and benevolent.			
23. **Teamwork**. Act with others towards a shared goal.			
24. **Self-respect**. Treat yourself with dignity and care, develop your self-awareness and self-esteem.			
Total:			

Add up the total number of marks in each column. Now think about your whole life. Write down your top three values (highest count) and look to reflect or apply those when confronted with a real situation.

Tool S1.8: Many Ways to Say "No"

Possible ways to say "No" and set boundaries.

- I have thought about it, thanks for your input, and the answer is no.
- We don't have money for that right now.
- We already have other resources we can use to manage this situation.
- That is outside the role you are employed for.
- The budget is tight, and we need that money for something else.
- Just no.
- Provide your reasoning and then say "No" and that you are not prepared to revisit the discussion.
- No sorry, no way.
- No and please do not ask me again.
- Can we clarify what I said earlier? What did you hear me say?
- I don't approve of it.
- I remember saying no.
- Perhaps you didn't hear me say we are not going to do that?
- I'm not going to be changing my mind about this.
- This conversation is over. I'm returning to other work now.
- It's okay to want something.

Tool S1.9: Assertiveness Tool

This tool gives you a framework to develop language about what you wish to assert. It also invites you to check in with yourself about your goal and if you think that it is right to be assertive about it. Write down your answers then stand up and say them say them to yourself without speaking. See what needs correcting.

- **A**ssess your rights and purpose in asserting your point of view.
- **S**et up the time and place to have the conversation.
- **S**pell out what happened.
- **E**xpress how you felt about it.
- **R**equest what you want them to do.
- **T**ell them what you will or will not do if they agree or don't agree.

Finally, check in with the person to hear what they have understood you to have said.

Section Two

Leading Others One-on-One—Helping Others Be the Best They Can Be

The words you speak today should be soft and tender for tomorrow you may have to eat them.

— Anonymous

2.1 The Story So Far—Understanding and Working with Others

Sam is now the leader of an Enterprise Portfolio Management Office (EPMO). She reports directly to the CEO. After Sam had met with her team one-on-one on the second day, she recognized that the team were eager, but they all seemed to be going off in different directions—some appeared to be heading in almost an opposite direction to what she understood was required and expected of the EPMO.

She realized that she had some serious work to do to develop rapport, build trust with each of her team members, and understand what had made them act in the manner they did. She needed to build agreements with each of the team that satisfied the needs of the organization and empowered the individual.

38 The Business of People: Leadership for the Changing World

Sam reviewed the personnel files and notes that had been left from her predecessor, which gave her a heads-up and good insight into the current situation for each of the team members.

Sam had a gut feeling, and as the days went by, it became clear to her that there was an issue which, if not dealt with, would become a potentially serious conflict and interrupt the work program. The issue seemed to be centered on a technical subject matter expert (SME) named Frankie. Frankie was inexperienced, relatively young, had low emotional intelligence (EI), and displayed overindulgence traits. Sam decided she would coach Frankie rather than transfer him, because Frankie had some very good technical skills that Sam recognized as valuable to the EPMO's objective.

Sam is aware that she can utilize a range of approaches and tools to develop Frankie, as well as others in the EPMO team. These approaches and tools are scalable, in that they can be used both in a one-on-one manner and also across groups.

2.2 Case Study

Recently, Madeleine worked with a serious situation that had started going badly from the person's first day on the job. This professional had started in the job and not been able to connect with the leader. She felt, in fact, that the leader was undermining her efforts. For example, they had an agreement about what time the day ended, which enabled the worker to pick up her child from school. But the leader had stopped her leaving on time for two days in a row in her first week, which set up a pattern of distrust. This was the first evidence of a large disconnect between leadership and staff.

This workplace situation ended with conflict and complaints and huge turmoil for staff and leaders, taking about two years to resolve and ending with the worker leaving the job. The cost to the business on so many levels was enormous.

In another case, a small business owner, who was also the CEO, would be unpredictable in his behavior. One minute he would be telling people off for not turning off their computers at night and wasting money. The next minute he would be showering people with small presents. Frequently, he had temper outbursts. This was mostly aimed at his secretary. At one time these outbursts were so bad that the turnover of secretaries was about three a year, and mostly he used the line from The Apprentice: "You're fired." No one was able to raise their concerns, because he was the boss and he would fire people as per the secretaries; people were scared but needed their jobs. Things went from bad to worse and the business didn't last long.

2.3 Solutions for the Situation

This section is focused on helping leaders understand and work with other humans. Bringing people with you as a leader requires you to build on your emotional intelligence skills (which we discussed in Section 1) and expand your social competence, which, when combined, are often referred to as the *soft skills*.

While emotional intelligence is defined as, "The ability to control your own emotions and respond effectively to others' emotions,"[*] Daniel Goleman goes on to speak of social competence as "more than just being chatty. These abilities range from being able to tune into another person's feelings and understand how they think about things." This helps you to be a great collaborator, a team player, and be effective in negotiations. In an article in 2012,[†] Goleman says, "All these skills are learned in life. We can improve on any of them we care about, but it takes time, effort, and perseverance. It helps to have a model, someone who embodies the skill we want to improve. But we also need to practice whenever a naturally occurring opportunity arises—and it may be listening to a teenager, not just a moment at work."

We will explore the approaches and skills that constitute social competence, building on the previous section on emotional intelligence.

2.3.1 Setting Up for Success

Planning Your Interactions—Using Three Primary Negotiations

This idea, which Madeleine learned from the late Colin McKenzie, is simple and, when applied to every situation in working with people, things will improve. Think of the three steps below as linear. First think about the nature of the relationship you want—whether there is high or low trust currently. Next work out how you, as two human beings on the planet, are going to work together. Before you delve into the substantive part of the conversation:

a. Relationship—develop it and understand it.

b. Agree on a process for working together (see Tool S2.3 on page 63).

c. Clarify the substance of the conversation.

---

[*] Goleman, 2010

[†] Goleman, 2012

Building Rapport

Rapport builds positive connection and engagement with another. It is a sense of emotional safety in which you can feel that you are being reassured as a person. To build rapport, you will need to adapt and talk in the other person's "currency." This is achieved by listening to them.

Start by being friendly and open, demonstrate warmth in your voice, smile, and find common ground. Take the time to learn names and pronounce them correctly. Acknowledge what the other person has said. Be nonjudgmental and share a little of yourself, while maintaining appropriate boundaries. Create an accepting environment by paraphrasing and asking questions to clarify understanding.

How do you know when rapport has been established? You will need to listen and observe carefully, because the tone of other person's voice may change, and you will recognize when they relax their body language and are, for the most part, genuine. There is also a flow to the conversation. They are engaged, present, and will share something of themselves or the situation and feel comfortable doing so.

However, rapport can be easily lost. These are some of the actions that people often inadvertently do:

- Getting the other person's name wrong or mispronouncing it

- Appearing uninterested/distracted by looking around—for instance, by looking at your phone or watch

- Not actively listening

- Doing too much talking, thus overpowering the conversation

- Pushing your personal agenda

- Asking closed questions, which impacts as being too pedantic

When you notice that you might have lost rapport with the person, think of what you might have done and apologize for that, then paraphrase what you have heard to this point. You might change the tone of your voice, shift your focus to the other person, and explore their needs. You could also seek feedback. Remember to smile and laugh when you are speaking with someone, and of course be honest, be genuine, and own what you can do.

Iain's HELP technique exemplifies this. He uses this simple yet very effective technique to build trust and to develop and maintain rapport. Naturally, it works better in some cases than in others; however, it demonstrates the "real"

Leading Others One-on-One—Helping Others Be the Best They Can Be 41

you and makes people inclined to like you more. This also assists greatly in beginning to influence people. See Section 3 for more on influencing. The HELP technique is as follows:

- **H**umor those involved.
- **E**xcite people.
- **L**isten to them as appropriate.
- **P**raise as often as you can when relevant.

A big concern for building rapport is the way we use our mobile phones. We recommend that for one-on-one or team meetings, you leave your phone away from your person. However, if you do need it on your person, then we recommend you switch it to silent with the vibration also off. That way, you can be fully focused on the person or persons you are wanting to build rapport with.

Having Empathy for Others

To be able to work well with others, you need to be able to be empathetic. This is the ability to observe and sense how others are feeling, showing you are interested in them, and recognize the range of emotions being displayed and respond appropriately. Daniel Goleman talks about the three kinds of empathy in his article *Empathy-101.**

1. **Cognitive empathy.** The ability to see the world through another's eyes—being able to understand how another person might think, which allows you to understand how to best communicate with this person. It helps you to work with those who are different.

2. **Emotional empathy.** Allows you to feel as if you were the other person. Tune into your own feelings and notice your body's reaction—this is how you recognize if you are in rapport and building a relationship or damaging it.

3. **Empathetic concern.** The demonstration of a person's concern for the other; at work it is about creating a safe working space, in which staff are supported to take risks and admit mistakes.

Your attitude to the person you are working with matters; if you do not think someone has anything important to say, then you will not want to listen to

---
* Goleman, 2013

42   The Business of People: Leadership for the Changing World

them, and therefore you will not be able to empathise. So how does one develop and practice the skill of empathy? Try these:

- Take an open-minded stance about the other party.
- Profoundly listen—be present and be interested.
- Understand the context.
- Listen for what is not being stated.
- Notice the tone of what has been said, because that will help your understanding of their feelings.
- Read facial expressions.
- Validate the right they have to hold their perspective.
- Acknowledge the content of the conversation and the feelings they express.
- Focus on the other person.
- Know there are three perspectives—yours, theirs, and the observers.

Empathy can be learned (but only if you have not been afflicted by Fetal Alcohol Syndrome). As a note, sympathy is different to empathy. Sympathy is feeling *what* the other person is feeling. With sympathy, you actually experience the feeling. That way you fall into their their life. Empathy is feeling *as if* you might think they would feel. But you are separate from their experience.

Your Attitude to Others

If we use an unconditionally constructive attitude (an idea developed by Fisher and Brown from the Harvard Law School Project on Negotiation[*]) for managing ourselves, we may find that we get along with people and manage tricky situations with finesse. We may also prevent any future conflict from occurring by using this approach.

For example, two acquaintances were walking together when one began complaining about a problem she was having with an estranged relative. The problem was causing her a lot of stress and discomfort, and she was blaming of the relative. The other considered what she had said and offered ideas about how to do things in a different way. The first became very upset and rude to the point of name calling and began to walk away. The second person then used this

---

[*] Fisher and Brown, 1989

unconditionally constructive attitude strategy, and the disgruntled person was able to reengage and have a useful and positive conversation.

Taking an unconditionally constructive attitude will help you to maintain a calm approach. This requires you to:

- Do only those things that are both good for the relationship and good for us, whether or not they reciprocate.

- Be rational yourself. Even if they are acting emotionally, balance emotions with reason.

- Listen to understand, not to reload. Even if they misunderstand us, try to understand them.

- Communicate with them even if they are not listening, and consult them before deciding on matters that affect them.

- Demonstrate reliability. Even if they are trying to deceive you, neither trust them nor deceive them—be reliable.

- Use non-coercive modes of influence. Even if they are trying to coerce you, neither yield to that coercion nor try to coerce them—be open to persuasion and try to persuade them.

- Accept them. Even if they reject us and our concerns as unworthy of their consideration, accept them as worthy of our consideration, care about them, and be open to learning from them.

Maintaining these attitudes can be hard to do but worth it.

Building Trust

In Section 1, we discussed strategies that intend to strengthen your leadership capability. These tie directly back to the 3P's to Success that was introduced in Iain's book *The Business of Portfolio Management—Boosting Organizational Value.* The 3P's to Success are supported by key leadership principles, leadership styles, and leadership techniques that together form a core leadership capability.

The ability to build trust with others stems from displaying six leadership principles. These are *self-mastery, power with people, persuasive communications, execution ability,* and *giving,* and when used consistently, they will encourage others to trust you. This is critical when change is being signaled, because change usually triggers uncertainty in others.

---

* Frazer, 2017

44   The Business of People: Leadership for the Changing World

To evoke trust from others, we need to be trustworthy ourselves. There are specific characteristics required to gain trust from others—*consistency, openness, honesty, loyalty,* and *respect.* These need to be paired with three levels of competence—namely, personal, technical, and organizational. The characteristics and competence levels blended together will provide you with trusting relationships that enhance smooth and efficient communications.

Without trust, the potential for lack of cooperation, misunderstandings, hidden agendas, and lack of motivation will be much higher. These are destructive to any working relationship and a huge risk to any leader, because they can destroy the relationship and seriously undermine culture with the individual, throughout the team, or across the organization.

There are some authors who stand out for their brilliant work that has become iconic. One of them is Patrick Lencioni who, in 2002, gave us *The Five Dysfunctions of a Team.*[*] In this book, the core of his story telling is that any high-performing working relationship must have a basis of trust in one another. Enough said—read the book, as millions of others have.

Being able to develop trust in others will not work, however, if you cannot trust them. In order to display trust yourself, you can show your vulnerability to others. Baroness Onora O'Neill, a philosopher and international justice and expert on developing trust, says that making yourself vulnerable implies that you trust the other person.[†] However, remember that the power of reciprocity then is evoked, and the other person is more likely to share something that is vulnerable to them. This allows trust to build, because you will speak of what is real, and you are building frankness and connectedness.

For a stepwise process to build trust, see Tool S2.1 on page 61.

Empowerment

Empowering others is a critical contributor of the 3P's to Success, in which the second "P" stands for people. There are certain behaviors a leader must display and deploy in order to empower others to act in a manner that is conducive to the desired outcome. These are *fostering collaboration* and *sharing power,* which, when combined, gain buy-in to shared objectives and strengthens the other person and team.

As a leader, you need to develop empowerment by fostering the following attributes in others:

---

[*] Lencioni, 2002

[†] O'Neill, 2013

- **A Sense of Purpose.** Goals, aspirations, persistence, hopefulness, and a sense of a bright future.

- **Social Competence:** The ability to elicit positive responses from others, thus establishing positive relationships with others.

- **Problem-Solving Skills**. Planning that facilitates seeing oneself in control and resourcefulness in seeking help from others.

- **Autonomy.** A sense of one's own identity and an ability to act independently and exert some control over one's environment.

Practically, this means that you are required to consider how you consistently demonstrate the above by ensuring:

- That in your everyday interactions with your people, they feel positive most of the time

- That your people feel they are fully contributing to problem solving and working together with others to solve pressing dilemmas

- That they have the sense they are autonomous individuals and can exert some control on their environment

- That there is hope and purpose in what they are doing that is meaningful to them and to the organization.

Sam recognizes that she needs to focus on building trust and rapport, then find ways to support empowerment for her team, especially Frankie.

To get alongside Frankie, her first action was to think of ways to do this. During a previous meeting, Frankie revealed an interest in racing drones. So, at the beginning of their one-on-one conversation, Sam disclosed her concern about a drone fault and a subsequent crash at a recent competition. This small exposure and request for ideas helped to build trust.

Sam also realizes, however, that she needs to make sure that Frankie is clear about the business objectives being pursued and at the same time stimulate the passion for individual excellence. Not an easy task.

Empowerment is not the same as delegation. The latter is often controlled by rules which can allow the person supposedly being empowered to feel frustrated due to bureaucracy and unwritten ground rules within the office. Sam has built trust and developed rapport and needs to be clear about expectations—creating an agreement with Frankie that is clear about how to account for the content and behavior of Frankie's contribution to the EPMO team and the wider organization.

46 The Business of People: Leadership for the Changing World

Creating Good Agreements with Each Other

A leadership trap that Madeleine frequently sees is that people feel let down or unhappy with the outcome of an interaction based on assumptions about expectations. As an example, a policy analyst voiced her concern about lack of decision making in her work group. What was discovered was that this expectation had not ever been clarified. Many "agreements" are unstated, and we only know that we have breached an "agreement" if we have the luck to have someone tell us straight up or if something goes wrong.

Clarifying these understandings by using the concept of "contracting" can be helpful. Contracting makes overt the expectations that we have of each other as we communicate.

An agreement, in Transactional Analysis (TA) terms, occurs when an "explicit, bilateral commitment to a well-defined course of action"* has been agreed. (Note that the agreement is about a plan of action, not necessarily what the outcome will be.)

According to Eric Berne,[†] considered to be the father of TA, there are three levels of contracting, as follows (these concepts have been further developed by Julie Hay in *Transactional Analysis for Trainers*[‡]):

- **Firstly, the procedural level.** Refers to the arrangements of the agreement—venue, timing, equipment, payment, etc.

- **Secondly, the professional level.** Understanding the aim of the work to be done and the competence of those entering into the contract to be able to carry out the work.

- **Lastly, the psychological level.** This refers to the often unspoken underlying aspect of the working relationship between people. It is based on mutual respect and trust. This last level is where we can sometimes get stuck, as usually we only know that this level has been breached when we are in trouble in the relationship.

To add further depth to understanding our agreements, there are four components which are deemed to be essential for a valid TA contract:

- **Mutual consent.** Both parties must agree to the contract, and this agreement is arrived at through negotiation. It means there is a specific offer

---

* Steward and Joines, 2002
† Berne, 2006
‡ Hay, 2009

and a specific acceptance with mutual effort to reach a conclusion. That is, all parties are clear on what they are entering into.

- **Consideration.** A form of exchange for time or work of one party for the other—for example, support and encouragement for delivering a full day's effort.

- **Competency.** Both parties are fully aware of the agreement that is being entered into and have the ability to perform the work outlined.

- **Lawful.** The goals and conditions must conform to the law and professional bodies—so, for example, in New Zealand, we are currently unable to enter into agreements for euthanasia.

A practical way to apply these ideas is to use the 6 P's of Process (see Tool S2.3 on page 63).

We know from influencing and negotiation theory that the more buy-in you have to the process, the more likely you will be to reach a robust and sustainable substantive outcome.

A useful tool is A Guide to Working with Me (see Tool S2.4 on page 64), which we think is a great way to start any working relationship. Complete the guide, and then take the time to talk with your staff, colleagues, or leaders about how you best work. You can also ask them to fill it out for themselves, and then you will have more information about them.

2.3.2 Supporting People

Impact and Intent

There can be a big difference between a person's intent and the impact they might have. For example, a middle manager whose intent was to have a quiet talk about a sensitive issue to gain insight from a competent staff member might say, "Can I take you aside?" The impact could very well be a scared reaction from the staff member. Her brain would tell her instantly there was an impending loss for her. The outcome would be that the staff member might react to the loss by having an amygdala hijack—being unable to think and reacting badly. The meeting would not be productive.

We imagine that this is not the response you would like to evoke in others, so it is useful to consider how you start a conversation. Recognize that your intention can be different to the impact that you have. No one person is at fault—it's just the way we work as humans, our script and frame of reference at play. If

The Business of People: Leadership for the Changing World

we are thoughtful, though, we can understand the disconnect between impact and intent.

As we go about our day, we normally do not plan to upset others; we are usually focused on doing our work and getting our job done. However, our behavior may unwittingly impact negatively on others. Being prepared to acknowledge that there is a difference between our good intent and a resultant negative impact is helpful. When we are working in a low-trust environment, we can begin by communicating our intent prior to our message delivery. This helps the listener understand the context of the message and is less likely to be filtered by the frame of reference. There are some microcommunication concepts that will help to create a better engagement and have your impact match your intent.

- Naming the purpose of your interaction.

- Framing—Consider starting with a positive collaborative statement, which will help the communication. We often do this as a normal part of our greetings: "Nice to see you again," said with a smile.

- Anchoring—How we begin a conversation matters, because people immediately decide if it is a loss or a gain for them. Being purposeful about the way we anchor the conversation can change the dynamic. For example, when delivering bad news, we may need to start with something that signals a loss, because then the person will be able to put on their psychological armor to help them cope with the situation. If we are delivering good news, support the moment by framing positively.

- Recognition of cognitive bias—All humans make judgments about others based on our upbringing, as per our frame of reference. To ensure that you understand how someone has interpreted what you have said, ask them to tell you what you have said. Ask an open question—for example, "What have you understood from what I have said?," not a closed question—for example, "Do you understand?" Rejoice when they tell you something unexpected—your plan to gain insight of their thinking has worked.

- Be consistence with your words and behavior.

Accountability

As a competent leader, you want to hold yourself and others accountable. This means having agreements to do so and systems that help keep tabs on the action. Being accountable is also facing up to the good and the bad, taking the rap as the leader, and not punishing people for their mistakes but not letting them off the hook either. Being able to hold people accountable includes the way people interact with each other, not just about the substance of the project you are working on.

Madeleine has been coaching a senior leader in an organization in which the rules and expectations are clear and yet the behaviors that are witnessed are appalling: Breaching agreements about being respectful by yelling, swearing, not attending meetings on time, ignoring some people's comments, punishing someone for unwittingly breaching an agreement while letting others off the hook for knowingly doing the same thing. Having the leadership courage to speak up and to raise awareness is key. It is in the everyday interactions that change can occur.

With the overindulgent world we are in now, fewer and fewer people are being held to account, and so when people come into the workplace and begin to be held accountable, it can be a confronting experience. Leaders will need to alter their interactions so new workers learn that being accountable is part and parcel of the culture—"the way we do things around here." Be patient and empathetic, because they really, truly don't know. (Use the Ladder of Accountability [Figure 2.1], first developed by J. D. Stewart in "The Role of Information in Public Accountability"[*]; see Tool S2.2 on page 62 for further explanation.)

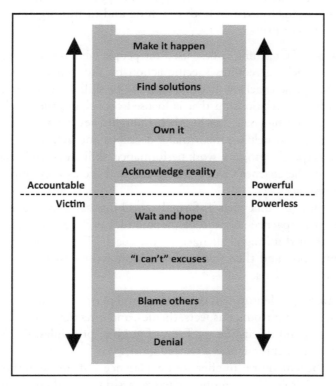

Figure 2.1 Ladder of Accountability

---

[*] Stewart, 1984

The Business of People: Leadership for the Changing World

As the leader, you are responsible. This means being clear with people about what they and others are responsible for and what you are responsible for. Sometimes these things do not become apparent until a bad or difficult situation occurs.

Coaching and Mentoring

We think it is useful to make a distinction between these two concepts, because we believe that too many people bracket coaching and mentoring together and use the term either in a singular manner or in a combined manner. This leads to confusion and the potential of a relationship breakdown between the person providing the service and the person receiving the service. We have a straight-forward definition of each term and offer these so you can use them in a one-on-one situation or in a team situation (albeit mentoring is not so effective in a team setting, whereas coaching is effective in both an individual as well as in a group setting). Underpinning both is the principle of trust. This needs to exist in both coaching and mentoring environments if success is to be confirmed.

- **Coaching.** Coaching is best used for people who are competent in their roles. Coaching requires specific action by the individual receiving the coaching (the coachee). It is not training or skill development. Coaching is built on a relationship that is focused on helping the coachee develop through setting goals, sharing their thoughts, testing and extending their thinking, and helping them make decisions and act. The coaching may address specific projects, work performance, skill areas, and general conditions in the coachee's work, workplace, and life as they impact on work performance.

  Although somewhat informal, coaching sessions are not relaxing chats; the coachee needs to be prepared for each session and be ready to have their thinking challenged by the coach. The coachee is expected to reflect upon and then follow through on actions that are agreed in the coaching sessions.

- **Mentoring.** Mentoring is oriented around perspective and associated dialogue. It can introduce aspects, themes, and directions to explore through thinking and discussion—a form of guiding principles, if you prefer, in which the mentor acts as a trusted guide.

  To be a mentor is to offer your experience and advice to those growing into their role. You can offer practical assistance and encourage mentees

Leading Others One-on-One—Helping Others Be the Best They Can Be 51

to broaden their horizons, embrace challenges, and set and achieve new goals. You may be able to invite the person being mentored to events and introduce them to networks to assist them in getting experiences and connections that will grow their abilities.

It is the desire that each mentee will take the skills, knowledge, and connections they have discussed, then reflect and apply those to the benefit of the organization and its business objectives.

Communication Skills

Engaging in purposeful communications is one of the most important duties any leader must perform. Being able to assess communication needs, plan to meet those needs, and effectively communicate information is a critical Volatile, Uncertain, Complex, and Ambiguous (VUCA) world skillset. Remember to consider both internal and external stakeholders who have an interest in your endeavors.

If you have experienced a miscommunication, then you know that perception creates different meanings to different people, and every day those differences in communication can cost you in terms of time, energy, and money.

One of the most overlooked aspects of communications is the number of channels that exist within any group. A simple and easy-to-remember formula ($n*n-1/2$, where n is the number of people in a team) assists greatly in determining the number of channels that exist in a team, department, or entire organization. As an example, Sam's team of five people in the EPMO gives a total of 10 communication channels to consider. However, one should note that the channel figure grows rapidly the bigger a team gets. This means that Sam also needs to think about the amount of time needed to ensure that there is enough allocated to each person in the quantity that is useful for both the group and the individual concerned.

Sam also knows that messages between communicator and receiver are often misinterpreted as a result of words used, physical expressions, tone of voice, frame of reference, and body language. The receiver may subconsciously use filters to create an interpretation of the message from the sender. She also knows that any type of communication can be distorted by "blockers" such as culture, distance, language, and noise. She understands that sending out email blasts to a large audience is not the manner likely to endear her to Frankie or the rest of the EPMO team. It will certainly not build trust either.

To combat the risk of miscommunicating through misunderstanding, Sam decides to again use the HELP technique as her base approach. In using this

52   The Business of People: Leadership for the Changing World

versatile technique, she uses **H**umor to get her points across, she seeks to **E**xcite the other person(s), she **L**istens and asks clarifying questions and acknowledges the responses received. She also uses genuine **P**raise at every opportunity. The versatility of the HELP technique creates a consistent and simple way for Sam to communicate and work with others in a one-on-one manner. Where necessary, it can be supplemented with one or more of the other techniques from this section.

Regardless of whether your communications are written or verbal, internal or external, formal or informal, vertical (up the organization hierarchy) or horizontal (across the organization hierarchy), your words, expressions, tone of voice, and body language have a considerable impact on how your message is interpreted and its meaning potentially distorted. Above all, the importance of being genuine and sincere on a consistent basis is a critical underlying attribute of any communication.

Remember to review your communication requirements to keep internal and external stakeholders informed and aligned. This can be achieved by identifying and grouping stakeholders, then understanding what communication tools are most effective in what circumstances. The creation of distribution of a functional and practical communications plan sets you up for success. However, sometimes times it is the micro skills that trip us up. Those micro skills are the understanding of what communication is, what vehicles we use, how we listen, how we ask questions to clarify, how we acknowledge other views, and how we behave.

You can go to the tools section to brush up the basics on your micro communication skills (see Tool S2.5 on page 66). This tool covers the four basic skills of:

- **Listening.** Being able to listen without reloading and to truly hear the whole of what someone is speaking about. Giving them time to finish.

- **Acknowledging.** Recognizing what others are communicating—feelings and substance. This is not necessarily agreeing.

- **Questioning.** Open and closed.

- **Advocating.** Making statements about what you want.

Many of us think that we are great at communicating, but mostly we are not, especially in pressured situations. We tend to overrate our own communication skills. Communication is message sent is message received. We cannot just rely these days on texts and/or email to ensure the message has arrived and been interpreted correctly. Yet often we do, and it is to our detriment. Build in communication loop checks to ensure the communication has been received. This

Leading Others One-on-One—Helping Others Be the Best They Can Be   53

seems like a time waster in a busy schedule—but it prevents miscommunications from happening.

Another key skill in communication is the power of observation. Being able to observe a situation well has many advantages—to be able to recognize what we are seeing, to be able to name what we are seeing without attribution or bias, to develop a body of knowledge about a situation, and to build confidence in our responses to situations. This will then help us in our communications with others and improve the quality of interactions within and around your organization.

To become accurate and efficient in your observation skills, you may need to train yourself. Begin by being quite pedantic—initially writing down what you observe and then going back and reflecting on it. There are various methods to use. One is a running record: Observe a situation or conversation for five minutes and record everything that you see. When you reflect on it, delete the judgment and impression words and rewrite as if you were a camera just doing the recording.

As you learn to observe, you can often become aware of the reasoning that you have provided for the situation (in that moment), but watch a little longer, and you may discover something more. Or you might then work to understand the behavior and discover a new take on the initial impression.

Another method is *time sampling*—during which you observe a situation throughout the whole day but only for five minutes each time. In addition, there is *event recording*—noting whenever a particular action occurs; *duration recording*—observing how long a situation lasts; *interval recording*—observing a specific behavior for a short time; *recording* (writing) your thoughts and feelings as they occur during the day, and this can be in relation to yourself or to your interactions with another.

What are you looking for when you are observing?

- Work competencies

- Thinking ability

- Feelings as they surface

- Behavior

- Interactions

- The use of language and communication patterns

As your power of observation improves, you will be able to notice trouble before it becomes unmanageable, prevent difficulties from arising, and intervene in a calm and peaceful manner when the need arises. You may also influence your reputation for the better.

54   The Business of People: Leadership for the Changing World

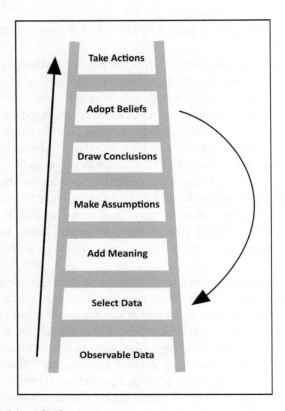

Figure 2.2   Ladder of Inference

A tool that combines observation with the communication skills of asking questions, acknowledging, and advocating is the Ladder of Inference (see Figure 2.2 above and Tool S2.6 on page 69 for the details).

Deception Detection

Because people coming into the workplace have different experiences and ways of operating, you will need to be able to observe whether there is deception occurring. Be observant, and particularly watch the person's eye movement. Typically, when a person is remembering, they will look in a different direction to when they are being creative—which is what being deceptive is. You will need to watch closely. Ignore smiles and watch above the nose. Of course, our responses may differ across cultures. In some cultures, lying is a culturally sanctioned life skill—it is held up and honored! Lastly, watch gross body language—by that we mean observe any body language that is inconsistent with what is being said.

What you observe is just that, an observation. Do not make accusations based solely on body movements. You will need to discuss what you have observed in a nonjudgmental manner in order to understand the other person's perspective. Use the Ladder of Inference to help you. Remember, all behavior makes sense to someone, and most people are not out to make a situation worse.

Understanding Currency

Being able to recognize the value that your staff or your own leader places on various aspects of their world and the working environment is useful to understand and will enhance your ability to communicate with them and to get your point across. Observe the interactions with those you are keen to work well with or those you want to influence and think about what they pay attention to. What do they value? Relationships, information, knowledge, status, time, statistics, strategy, detail? Think of working, learning, and thinking style preferences. Listen and observe.

Once you have an idea of what is important to them, consider how to deliver your message. Do you go in with a dilemma or a problem? To get their advice or to blame? Do you come armed with options? Do you provide enough or too much context? Do you provide too much or too little detail?

If they are concerned about time and you deliver a backstory for 20 minutes, you will not have a receptive audience. How you get your message across can sometimes matter more than the content of the message. If you are not communicating well—think about how you are delivering it.

2.3.3 Daily Details and Corrections

Ego States: Understand the Parent, Adult, and Child Model

To support you in being the best you can be, consider reflecting on the idea of ego states. Are you functioning in the present as a parent, child, or adult? You can recognize this by the system of thoughts, feelings, and behaviors that you have. If you are feeling pushed to behave like a child, it may mean that the other person is functioning from their parent ego state. If you are feeling like an adult and then someone wants to have fun—you might join them, and the playful part of your child will come out to play also.

These ideas come from Eric Berne, author of *Transactional Analysis in Psychotherapy: A Systematic Individual and Social Psychiatry.*[*] Berne is a psychiatrist and psychoanalyst who went on to develop a theory of human interaction, or TA. His basic premise is that:

- People are OK.
- Everyone deserves positive recognition.
- People decide their own destiny and have the power to change these decisions at any time.

He mentions that each one of us has in ourselves, a parent, an adult, and a child ego state. This can be represented by Figure 2.3:

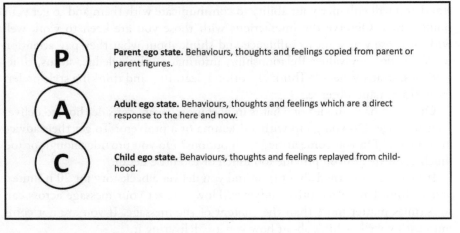

Figure 2.3 Ego State Diagram

TA is a way of understanding how each of us interacts with others. The way we transact within these ego states makes up our communication patterns.

When we get stressed, it is easier for us to move out of our present adult self and behave in ways that lead to more difficult interactions. Support yourself to make sure that you as the leader stay in the "present" and in your adult ego state and work to support that others are also. Being an adult in the workplace is a helpful state to be in. With the impact of overindulgence in the world, many young people are coming into the workplace not operating as adults. You will need to lead and support these young people as they grow into their competent selves.

---

[*] Berne, 2016

Many people who have been overindulged as children appear to be as a child would be—their voices are high pitched and soft, they like being the center of attention, they have a free spirit and can become upset very easily.

Decision Making

A good leader supports her people to make decisions and to take the decisions she needs to make in a timely way. It is also useful to delay decisions if that becomes necessary, and the key step here is to communicate that you need to. When you think about your work life, notice the decision-making patterns you have held (see Fig. 2.4). As you proceed, check your decision patterns against any agreements that exist. Are you really empowering your people?

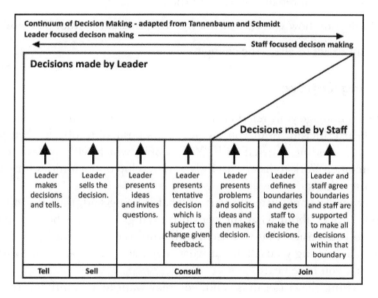

Figure 2.4   Continuum of Decision-Making Behavior

What seems most important is the communication over the type of decision making you have chosen for that situation.

Mistake Making

We all make mistakes; we would not be human if we did not. The question is, how do we minimize their impact? Managing the consequences of a mistake and the trouble that might ensue in the organization is important, but the

58   The Business of People: Leadership for the Changing World

damage that the mistake might have made to the relationships is vital to your enterprise's success. Ensuring that your skill set includes tools for repairing after a mistake has been made will aid your potency as a leader.

Here is a quick guide on how to repair a mistake you have made:

- Be open to hearing that a mistake has been made.
- Respond calmly to your awareness.
- Recognize your contribution to the mistake.
- Make an apology to those who have been harmed.
- Consider options to fix the problem.
- Take steps to repair the harm to the relationship.
- Reflect on how you can ensure that that mistake cannot be made again.
- Plan to act to effect the changes.

Managing Criticism

In order to manage your relationships with others, you need to be able to listen to and hear criticism. If all you are getting is positive feedback, then possibly you are surrounding yourself with "Yes" people, which will not lead to a good final outcome. Work to listen carefully and develop opportunities for people to easily raise criticism.

Sometimes we only listen to part of what is being said, then begin to create our own "story" about what the person is saying. Instead, when the person is talking to you, ensure that you listen fully until they have finished, then check what you are telling yourself about what they have said, and clarify with them about what you have heard.

If you think the criticism is valid, you may want to act on that information. However, when you receive criticism that does not make sense, do not automatically think of excuses, tell the person they are wrong, or even apologize. Instead begin by acknowledging that the critic might be right, and consider what to do about fixing the situation. You might need more information, especially if you cannot understand the motive of the giver, or when you think you haven't heard the whole story. It may help to dig a little deeper by asking open-ended questions, requesting specific examples.

It may also be that there is no validity in their statements—in that case you may wish to use these strategies. Fogging is used to deal with situations that are non-constructive, have intense criticism, or are being delivered in a highly emotional manner. You may agree with some of the trivial points or you may

Leading Others One-on-One—Helping Others Be the Best They Can Be 59

partially agree. Say nothing else while mentally sticking to your own point of view. You can then reply with:

- "You may be right."
- "That could be so."
- "Oh, I don't like that much either."

This can cool the situation by taking the wind out of someone's sails.

You can also postpone the discussion to another time if you feel that you are not up to listening at this point. This is useful when the interaction is too aggressive or at an impasse, or when either of you needs to be calmer to think. Be sure you arrange a new time.

Or, you might prefer to suspend judgment before you respond, giving yourself time to check your own feelings, needs, and thoughts, then prepare a reply.

Being Able to Apologize

Being a leader means we need to know how to apologize. Just saying, "Sorry," is not enough. In order to make an apology, you need to be aware that you have transgressed from, for example, your values, an agreement, an objective. Your powers of observation can be very useful here in our busy world, where we can easily discount the signals that are all around us. Secondly, you must decide that it is important for the relationship now and into the future that you repair the harm or perceived harm. Much trouble has occurred after a small incident and no acknowledgement has been made. Take the time—it is worth it. Here is a checklist of items to consider when making an apology:

- Acknowledge what has happened and your part in it.
- Acknowledge the hurt and the pain your action has caused.
- Explain how you are not going to do it again to them or anyone else.
- Acknowledge the underlying reasons behind the actions.
- Say what you are doing to ensure that the underlying issues are being dealt with.
- Clarify how you are going to maintain the new direction.

Performance Discussions

As a leader, you will be providing real-time feedback and information about what is going well and what is not to all your direct reports on a frequent basis, so that nothing will be a surprise during the year when you hold formal performance conversations (if they are even a thing any more). You will be working with adults and treating them as adults, fully able to learn from these conversations. The skill/will matrix can help to assist you to decide what kind of conversation you will have (see Fig. 2.5). Tess Conran-Liew has included this framework in her book *Working in a Group*,[*] about leading and relating co-operatively.

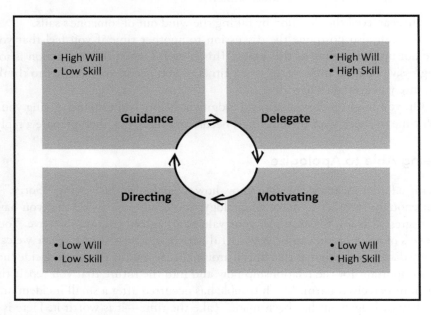

Figure 2.5 Skill/Will Matrix Diagram

Exiting Persons

Surely one of the most challenging tasks of any leader is the exiting of people from one's team or the wider organization. Unless it is based on severe misconduct, the situation is a very difficult one and often can have legal implications, depending on the labor laws of the country you are in. The difficulty comes from either a legal perspective, a performance perspective, or a change perspective. Leaders must strive to ensure that the person or persons exiting leave in a dignified manner, including being crystal clear about the reasons why. If the person(s) leaving can exit with a positive view of the organization, then this is a good thing for the brand. In our view, all leaders must find time to meet the person(s) face-to-face and have the exit conversation in that manner. This is

---

[*] Conran-Liew, 2004

Leading Others One-on-One—Helping Others Be the Best They Can Be 61

not always practical, however, but is far better than some standard form letter from a faceless HR person that doesn't even have a signature. That is not good enough in terms of accountability and is a considerable detriment to organizational culture.

2.4 Case Study—Using These Ideas for Success

Madeleine became interested in working with people to resolve conflict following a situation within an organization. Two people who had worked together for over 10 years each approached her separately, because they had trouble working with each other. This puzzled Madeleine, as her experience of working with both people was lovely. Neither person could understand how they had gotten into the situation they were in. In the individual (confidential) meetings, Madeleine discovered that something had occurred the week they both started: Person A (Andy) had been told by Person C (Chris) to be wary of Person B (Blake). Chris also told Andy that Blake disliked them. Of course, this left Andy cautious and not forthcoming, and Blake found Andy to be prickly and non-trusting.

Blake explained that this was not the case—Blake in fact admired Andy's work and didn't understand why they couldn't form a good working relationship. With this information, Madeleine was able to ask them both questions about this perspective during their joint meeting. When the answers were delivered, both parties understood what had happened, and 10 years of "trouble" fell away. Within about 15 minutes, they stood up and said, "Lets go and have a coffee." They had it sorted. Emotional intelligence and social competence are real things, and they pay big dividends.

2.5 Tools

Tool S2.1: Developing Trust—Time Structuring*

When this six-step process is actioned, you can build trust. It helps you to know exactly what to do in any given situation.

1. Time alone—this enables you to focus on what you are there to do.

2. Rituals—as you greet others or begin a meeting having a standard ritual helps people to predict and so feel safe. For example, a hand shake, hugs, kisses, prayer, or a hongi.

---

* Stewart, I. and Joines, V. (2002)

62   The Business of People: Leadership for the Changing World

3. Pastiming—Pass time by talking general chit chat but without action results; for example, the weather, sport, topics of general conversation. This allows people to test and assure themselves that it is safe, as you cannot "get it wrong."[*]

4. Doing the activity (working or playing) that you have gathered to do

5. Psychological games—this is the equivalent to moving through the storming stage of Tuckman's theory[†]—here we understand where the power is and what is safe and not safe.

6. The last stage is being able to be truly authentic—being able to express what really matters in order to resolve concerns and problems. This is an exchange of authentic wants and needs. Not being able to do this often means people are not able to solve the real problem.

If we want to deliberately build trust in a conversation or a group, we can do this by creating interactions that move from 1 through to 6. A point to note is that many interactions get stuck is at level 5. To move beyond level 5, we need clear contracting about what you will or will not do. Stay present in your adult self, and be communicative about what you are asking for and what you are offering the other person.

Tool S2.2: Ladder of Accountability (See Fig. 2.1 on page 49)

We can hold ourselves or others accountable by reflecting on our behavior and our thinking. When you are in a difficult situation, consider how you think about it: Are you able to acknowledge the reality you are in and own it—good or bad—then find solutions to the problem before acting to reach a resolution? If so, you are accountable and powerful and display above-the-line behavior. However, if you are waiting and hoping, making excuses for yourself, blaming others, or not acknowledging there is even an issue—then you will feel like a victim and are powerless.

It is your choice to be above or below the line. If you often see yourself below the line, then seek help to change. It is possible.

Madeleine has recently been working with a group in which one person is leaving and is confused and distressed. Madeleine learnt that the person's behavior has been problematic for others for years, but no one has had the straight conversation.

Notice how this often plays out in everyday interaction.

---

[*] Stewart and Joines, 2002

[†] Tuckman, 1965 and 1977

Leading Others One-on-One—Helping Others Be the Best They Can Be   63

Tool S2.3: The 6 P's of Process—Process Preparation Sheet

The 6 P's	My plan
1. Purpose *Why are you meeting?* To understand people's different perceptions? To exchange information? To brainstorm options and ideas? To motivate key people? To decide on an action plan? To reach an agreement?	
2. Product *What do you want to have at the end?* Notes for personal use? List of questions to follow up on? Draft memorandum for others? Process or framework agreement? Concrete tasks? Signed agreement? Agreements for the next meeting?	
3. People *Decide who should be at the meeting based on the purpose and product.* Family members? Advisors/accountants? Kaumatua/Kuia/Elders? Colleagues? Experts/managers? Clients? Outside consultants? Third party facilitator/mediator? What roles do participants take—facilitator, time keeper, recorder	

(continues on next page)

64   The Business of People: Leadership for the Changing World

Tool S2.3: The 6 P's of Process—Process Prep. Sheet (cont.)

4. Procedures *How are you going to run this meeting?* Do you need some safety agreements? How long is the meeting for? Who is going to talk first? How are you going to decide? What is on the agenda? How long are you meeting for?	
5. Place *Where is the meeting going to take place?* Face to face? Over the phone? Emails? Venue—home, marae, offices, community room? Café? Walking conversation?	
6. Psychological safety *Do I trust them or myself in this situation?* Low trust? What boundaries do we have? How can I manage my self-care? What concerns do I have for their psychological safety? What might I do?	

While you can plan for these 6 P's in your preparation, it is more effective to influence others by having them collaborate with you about the 6 P's before you begin the conversation/intervention.

Tool S2.4: A Guide to Working with Me

Use the knowledge that you have of yourself to complete this guide, then invite those you work with to complete it. The third step is to discuss who you both are and then build some agreements to help you work effectively together.

Leading Others One-on-One—Helping Others Be the Best They Can Be 65

Part 1: Values and Ethics	My Values About It . . .
For example: The principles that I think need to be applied to my work are . . .	Excellence in everything and a "can-do" attitude
The reason I work in this organization doing this job is because I believe . . .	
These are the things I value the most about working with people.	
These are the things I value the most about the content of our work.	
My goals for my role are . . .	

Part 2: My Learning Preferences	How I Process Information . . .
For example: Random/sequential Concrete/abstract Visual/auditory/kinesthetic/spatial Introvert/extrovert Big picture/small details	

Part 3: My Behavior	This Is How I Will Behave:
When I am really stressed I will . . .	
When I am disappointed I will . . .	
I expect you to . . . when you want to give me feedback	
When I want to celebrate your successes, I will . . .	
When I am confused about what is happening, I will . . .	
When I am angry, this is how I will behave . . .	
When I am rushing, I frequently . . .	

(continues on next page)

66   The Business of People: Leadership for the Changing World

Tool S2.4: A Guide to Working with Me (cont.)

When you need some time to talk to me, I would prefer that you	
When you work with me, I would like you to use this process when I make a mistake . . .	

Tool S2.5: Basic Communication Skills Checklist

Listening

Listening involves three skills: *attending, using minimal encouragers,* and *acknowledging.* The following provides a checklist for your use.

- **Attending** is about being truly present with the person who is talking. This behavior is decreasing in our society, and so providing this can be compelling for your people:

  o Listen "actively."

  o Clarify what the person has said.

  o Reflect back, demonstrating that you have understood what the person has said.

  o Attend to their emotion.

  o If via phone—smile.

  o Notice your posture—it reflects your energy.

  o Be present—fully there.

  o Budget the time.

  o Take away actions.

  o Be aware of the anxiety you hold about the time you are spending on the phone.

- **Using minimal encouragers** to talk—these help the person who is talking to know you are still there and listening carefully to them. These are usually a natural part of a conversation.

  o Encouraging sounds—for example, "mmh," "ahh," etc.

Leading Others One-on-One—Helping Others Be the Best They Can Be   67

- o Bridging the conversation: Put in little bits of information, or say "so . . . ," "then . . . ," "and . . . ," and allow the space for the person to continue. They are important to encourage the caller to communicate.

- o Paraphrasing/summarizing.

- o Fostering good rapport and relationships.

- o Using positive language/contacts/web links to be proactive.

- o Reassurance—closing the communication loop, supporting the caller to know the matter will be taken care of.

- o Provision of appropriate resources.

- o Using appropriate cultural terms and being culturally aware.

- o Active listening and recording notes for future reference (you and others) and reflection on what you could have done differently.

- o Knowing what specific information from a range of situations needs to be provided to students to help them.

- **Acknowledging**—lets a person know you have heard them; it provides information back to the talker about what they have said and the impact on them, both substantively and emotionally:

- o Vocal feedback: "uh huh," "sure," "mmm,hmm" (only use this if you do agree with what they have said).

- o Keeping it simple.

- o Statements—"I understand this is hard/new . . . ," "You have said . . . and this had left you feeling . . ."

- o Smiling.

- o Demonstrating you have heard the feelings and the nuances.

- o Recognizing the person and their situation.

- o Repetition—sometimes you need to say the same thing many times.

Naming Feelings and Emotions

Being able to name feelings and emotions accurately is useful in managing conversations because it can save you a lot of time and them a lot of anguish. If you name their feeling, they do not need to keep telling you the story, because you

68   The Business of People: Leadership for the Changing World

have got "it." Paul Ekman's Atlas of Emotions* is a great tool for understanding and developing a vocabulary of emotions.

Also, naming your own feelings helps you to recognize your own state, and that will help you to regulate and to choose what you want to do with your emotions. Knowing that our emotions come from our thinking, and because we are in change of our thinking, we can then negotiate how we feel at any given time.

Asking Questions

- *Open questions*: The art of asking open questions is to support people to talk rather than to ask questions to solve your own problem. Asking open ended questions:

  o Provides an opportunity for the talker to give more perspective

  o Helps to build rapport

  o Start with the Where, When, Who, What, Why, and How?

  o Use the pyramid of intensity to think about your questions. Begin with:

  o Where, who, when—gathers the data; then

  o What and how—gets the opinion/ideas of the speaker; lastly

  o Why—drills into objectives, beliefs, and values.

- *Closed questions*—usually a yes or no or one-word response.

  o Are good for getting consent and confirmation or commitment to some aspect you have been discussing.

  o Allows the talker to give one-word answers.

  o Unless it is to get the facts, closed questions can be unhelpful.

Note—saying "tell me . . ." is not a question and often elicits a negative reaction. "Tell me" is, in fact, a command and unconsciously suggests a power stance. This will be the reason you may get the reaction. Ask the same thing with an open question and you will most likely see a different result.

Advocating

This is the skill of being able to be assertive. (See Tool S1.9 on page 36.)

---

* Eckman, 2019

Leading Others One-on-One—Helping Others Be the Best They Can Be   69

Tool S2.6: Ladder of Inference (see Fig. 2.2 on page 54)

Adapted from work by S. I. Hayakawa[*] as elaborated by Chris Argyris and Don Schon,[†] the Ladder of Inference helps to clarify a way to communicate with people to understand others. We can use the ladder to:

- Help test our assumptions.

- Be clear with others about their reasoning.

- Be clear with others about your reasoning.

- Understand how and why different people come to different conclusions using the same data.

- Explore how we have come to different views.

- Look for common ground.

The ladder rests on the ground of all available data. When we make decisions, we move up the ladder until we're ready to take action.

- On the first rung, we *select data*—we pay attention to some of the information and ignore other information that is available to us, based on our frame of reference and our script.

- On the second rung, we *make assumptions*—based on the data selected and our experience, we anticipate events or reactions related to those assumptions.

- On the third rung, we *draw conclusions and formulate beliefs,* based on those assumptions.

- On the last rung, we *act* based on what we now call our truth.

Using the ladder: We suggest the use of a simple question technique similar to the following. Some questions that could be used:

- What information did you (I) consider?

- Is there other data that I (you) considered that you (I) didn't?

- Why didn't you (I)?

- What did that data tell you (me)?

- What assumptions did I (you) make?

---

[*] Hayakawa, 1939

[†] Argrys and Schon, 1985

70 The Business of People: Leadership for the Changing World

- How did you (I) come to that conclusion?

- Why do I (you) believe that?

The intention behind such questions is not to judge your assumptions, conclusions, or actions—or those of others. The intention is to help make more visible and clear the thinking processes that led to them.

Why we sometimes get into trouble by:

- Not spending enough time at the bottom of the ladder, examining the data.

- Not testing the assumptions that we make or have been made—some may be so pervasive and ingrained in our thinking that we experience them as universally true.

- We are unable to stay open to the genuine spirit of inquiry and reflection.

An interesting point is that when we adopt a belief, we then can only select data that reinforces that belief.

Section Three

Managing Groups— Working Together for Great Outcomes

The attitude of the leader will determine the attitude of the pack.

— Colin Thompson*

3.1 The Story So Far—People Behave Consistently in Groups

Sam pursues and secures a new role as leader of the operations group within his organization. His title is now Chief Operations Officer (COO). It has been four years since he began leading the Enterprise Portfolio Management Office (EPMO). His promotion is based on merit and via a referral from the existing CEO.

The role became available after the incumbent COO left for another organization. Sam's selection and appointment were due to the display of his leadership skills and his ability to work well with people. He is now part of the executive group and realizes that he has a marvelous opportunity to demonstrate his people leadership capabilities further to a wider audience—including the board of directors, if he performs well on the right things at the right time. He decides

---
*

72 The Business of People: Leadership for the Changing World

that a focus on value and value management will allow him to set a new purpose for the department. He also decides to empower his people further and drive a performance-oriented environment.

While his previous leadership successes were noted and praised, he realizes that this role has much more responsibility and associated challenges. Considering the operations group size and number of people employed and the complexity of the issues his group is facing, he knows that the people will be the key to further success. He needs to keep using the tools and techniques learnt previously but also gain additional skills and knowledge of strategies and systems. Sam is aware of a recent horror story on leadership fraud from a rival organization which led to the brand of the organization being severely tarnished and court cases required to be resolved.

Sam needs to quickly assess his direct reports and gain an understanding of the group dynamics both within this leadership team and also across the whole group. He is certain that most of the work performed by the group will be within a program-of-work and/or project style. Therefore, the structure, composition of the teams, and group dynamics will be critical for the sustained high-performance output that he desires. We will see how Sam scales many of the approaches mentioned in the previous sections—for example, social and emotional intelligence, individual styles; thinking, learning, working, and communication skills.

3.2 Case Study

A few years ago, a New Zealand technology-based organization approved a business case to invest in a new operations business system that would allow for greater efficiency to be captured. The existing system was very old and had limited functionality for capitalizing on the digital age. The Chief Information Officer (CIO) was made the official sponsor on behalf of the organization, and an initial budget of $45 million was made available. The organization had a parent company in the United Kingdom and a regional office in Australia. One of the first decisions that the CIO made was to engage a large external consulting firm to be the program-of-work manager and team. This team quickly grew and numbered around 50–60 people on a regular basis. They were blended with a large number of people from different business units to form what should have been a cross-functional team.

They failed to deliver. The consulting firm had a technology understanding but lacked the necessary program-of-work skills to drive the initiative to an outcome. Time was passing, and the budget was being consumed quickly. Iain was asked to do a review and found that a significant reset was required for

Managing Groups—Working Together for Great Outcomes 73

the program of work to have any chance of success. Worse was the low morale exhibited by the wider team. They had had the energy sucked out of them.

The consultant organization tried to defend their position but failed in that also. Included in the turnaround plan was a wider team off-site gathering at which aspects of the reset could be diagnosed, planned, and prioritized over a three-day period. The CIO arranged to invite the regional CEO to do a "morale-lifting" presentation in person, with the intention of re-motivating the wider team and the program of work. This was scheduled for day one of the forum.

On the morning of the first day, some 100 people had gathered in the off-site venue and awaited the arrival of the CEO. He was running late. Eventually, he and his entourage arrived, with him on his mobile phone speaking quite loudly and heard by the gathered audience to say, ". . . and your call is important to me. I have to do something here first; however, it will be quick as it is not much of a priority." You could hear the room sag and the reaction of people, who had been excited and eager, was that they had the energy sucked out of them again. Any respect and trust they had for the CEO was gone in a moment.

Without doubt, this was the worst example of leadership on several fronts that Iain has witnessed. The program of work eventually delivered a substantially reduced scope for a significant budget overspend. The CEO resigned soon after, and the CIO resigned a month or so later.

Preventing these types of disasters is possible. In order to be able to lead well, you must understand how people operate as individuals and in groups. This means learning the art of leading groups. This is a changeable, constantly moving target, but there are concepts and tools to learn and use.

3.3 Solutions for the Situation

We are going to describe a range of solutions that will support you and your groups to work well.

- First we will address the life cycle and nature of groups, the building blocks for groups to function well, and then agreements to align the members.

- We will then talk about group structures and how to choose the correct group structure for the outcome you are seeking.

- Then we will describe skills that you will be required to use (or have someone else use for you) to ensure that the group works well.

- Finally, we will discuss a range of support mechanisms that can ensure your groups flourish.

3.3.1 Life Cycle of Groups
From Forming to Adjourning

The processes by which a team is established, develops, and performs has been studied by many people. The work done in the 1960s and added to in the 1970s by researchers Bruce Tuckman and Mary Jensen still has significant relevance today, especially in a program of work or project management environment.

Tuckmans original 1960s[*] model shows how team development passes through four phases of development, as shown in Figure 3.1, from initially forming, then storming, norming, and performing ideally right through to the fifth stage, added in the 1970s,[†] when the team disbands, hence the reference to "mourning." The developmental journey is characterized by three factors—namely, *content* (what the team or group aims to achieve), *process* (how the team intend to work), and *feelings* (the environmental/emotional situation that exists).

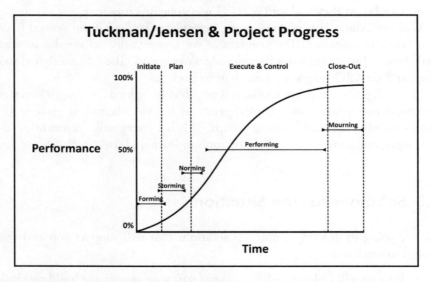

Figure 3.1 Tuckman/Jensen Model with Project Stages. (Adapted from Tuckman/Jensen Model[†])

The characteristics of each stage and leadership dependency needed are outlined in the sections below and Table 3.1. Tuckman described the distinct stages that a group or team can encounter as it comes together and starts to operate.

---

[*] Tuckman, 1965
[†] Tuckman and Jensen, 1977

This process can be subconscious, although an understanding of the stages can help any group move through each stage more quickly and less painfully.

- **Stage 1: Forming.** Individual behavior is driven by a desire to be accepted by others and avoid controversy or conflict. Serious issues and feelings are avoided, and people focus on being busy with routines, such as team organisation, who does what, when to meet, etc. But individuals are also gathering information and impressions—about each other and about the scope of the task and how to approach it. This is a comfortable stage to be in, but the avoidance of conflict and threat means that not much actually gets done. There is also a reliance on the leader to provide direction and support on the objective and expected outcomes.

- **Stage 2: Storming.** Individuals in the group can only remain nice and polite to each other for so long, as important issues start to be addressed. Some people's patience will break early, and minor confrontations will arise that are quickly dealt with or glossed over. These may relate to the work of the group itself or to roles and responsibilities within the group. Some will observe that it is good to be getting into the real issues, while others will wish to remain in the comfort and security of the Forming stage. Depending on the culture of the organisation and individuals, the conflict will be more or less suppressed, but it will be there, under the surface. To deal with the conflict, individuals may feel they are winning or losing conflict discussions and will look for structural clarity and rules to prevent the conflict persisting. When individuals leave or join the group, there may be a return to this stage.

- **Stage 3: Norming.** As Stage 2 evolves, the rules of engagement for the group become established, and the scope of the group's activities and responsibilities is clear and agreed. Having had their arguments, they now understand each other better and can appreciate each others' perspective, skills, and experience. Individuals listen to each other, appreciate and support each other, and are prepared to change preconceived views: They feel they're part of a cohesive, effective group. However, individuals have had to work hard to attain this stage and may resist any pressure to change—especially from the outside—for fear that the group will break up or revert to the Storming stage.

- **Stage 4: Performing.** Not all groups reach this stage, characterised by a state of interdependence and flexibility. Everyone knows each other well enough to be able to work together and trusts each other enough to allow independent activity. Roles and responsibilities change according to need in an almost seamless way. Group identity, loyalty, and morale are all

76 The Business of People: Leadership for the Changing World

high, and everyone is equally task oriented and people oriented. This high degree of comfort means that all the energy of the group can be directed towards the tasks and objectives at hand. A leader needs to maintain a focus on attaining and maintaining this stage so that consistent levels of high performance are achieved.

- **Stage 5: Adjourning (Mourning).** This last stage is about completion and disengagement, both from the activity conducted and from other group members. Individual team members will feel a sense of pride in having achieved much and will be delighted to have been part of such an enjoyable group. They need to recognize what they have done and consciously move on. Some commentators describe this stage as the "mourning" stage, in recognition of the sense of loss felt by each member as they depart the group.

It is useful to know that each time a group changes—when a member exits or a new person enters—then the group process is likely to rebound or recycle. Therefore, spending time with incoming team members and exercising the team agreement together with an ongoing focus on the outcome will minimise any disruption. Remember, any rebound is the nature of the group dynamic; people are not being difficult for the sake of it—even if it feels like that to you as the leader. Table 3.1 summarizes the interactions of group members during each stage.

Building Blocks for Successful Teams

Along with the knowledge of how groups work as a life cycle, it is helpful to be aware of the key components for a successful group or team (See Fig. 3.2). Developing the structure with the group if it is new or informing those coming into an established group means that group participants or team members have clarity and, therefore, a level of psychological safety. This means they can think and work well. No one has to operate from the fight-or-flight part of their brain.

These can be included in a Team Agreement (see next section) and, hopefully, supported by the existing organizational culture. A specific charter document for each initiative that outlines the scope of the initiative will assist in the understanding of the parameters of the output required and outcome expected.

Team Agreements

Diversity in our organizations and teams is increasing considerably and is now a focal point for many leaders. Because of this, we cannot make assumptions

Table 3.1 Tuckman/Jensen Team Development Stages

Direction of Development

	Forming	Storming	Norming	Performing	Adjourning (Mourning)
Characteristics	Unclear about purpose Uncommitted Cautious Dependent on direct leadership	Conflict Confusion about objectives Independent and polarising behavior Forming of cliques	Purpose, objectives are clearer Come to agreements More confident Interdependent behaviour	Members take full responsibility for tasks Members take initiative Members facilitate themselves Members work proactively Members have fun	Closure Sadness Separation
Leadership Needed	Mostly directive	Mostly coaching	Mostly facilitating	Mostly delegating	Mostly facilitating
Leadership Primary Actions	Build Rapport Build Trust Influencing	Coaching Guiding Communicating	Encouraging Guiding Communicating	Enhancing Sustaining Communicating	Thanking Celebrating Communicating
Team Reaction to Leadership	Tentative	Challenging	Supporting	Supportive, shared responsibility	Collegial/supportive
The team members want to know:	Where do I fit in?	What are the priorities? Who is in charge of what?	What is next?	Who is the best person for this task or role? How can I contribute?	Where do I go now? What happens to me?

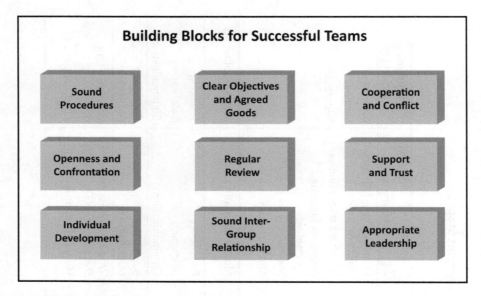

Figure 3.2 Building Blocks for Successful Teams

that we all think the same way or respond to situations in a way that makes sense to others.

A very useful tool that we have used successfully many times is a Team Agreement, sometimes referred to as a *team charter* or even a *team contract*. A Team Agreement is a set of guidelines that each team member contributes towards and agrees to respect and work by. It typically includes the commitments each team member is making to the team, working ground rules, meeting guidelines and procedures, problem solving, decision making, feedback tools, ways to manage conflict, and any other guidelines the team feels would be useful in keeping the team on track and relationships between team members strong. The core purpose is to agree on ground rules for daily work that all team members follow.

The items included in Team Agreements are focused on how people work together, not what they are working on—that is, a program-of-work plan, project management plan, or similar.

It is important that the team agreement is created as soon as possible after the team is formed and that it is reviewed every time a new member joins the team. The team leader has an important role in making sure the agreement is always alive and current. The team members should create the agreement with some guidance/facilitation from the team leader. When completed, each team member and the team leader should commit to working together by signing the agreement. In signing the agreement, each individual offers a form of pledge for the duration that the team is together.

Once the team has agreed on how they will work together, they need the skills and tools to raise concerns with others if there has been a perceived breach of the team's agreements. In Section 2, we discussed the Ladder of Accountability (see page 49). Perhaps upskilling workshops in dealing with difficult conversations or other needs could be offered. Whatever approaches you choose, always ensure that the team has opportunities to practice in giving each other positive and corrective information that will help the team function at its best.

It is most likely that any group formed will need to interface with other groups and other stakeholders, both inside and outside the organization. As mentioned previously, there are many channels of communication that occur in any team. A stakeholder management plan is critical to have in this situation, so that a satisfactory level of contracting can be achieved and relied upon. For example, the numbers of contracts can play out as in Figure 3.3, each needing its own agreement.

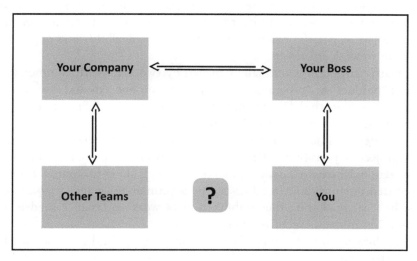

Figure 3.3 Four-Cornered Contract

In Figure 3.3, for example, your company has talked to your manager about you doing some work, and your manager then talks to you about that. Others have also talked to other teams. Then you come along and talk to the other teams with your understanding in your head. You push on and do the work with your team. If all goes well—and luck is on your side—the work gets well done. More commonly, however, you have a slightly different interpretation

80   The Business of People: Leadership for the Changing World

and version of events than the team and things quickly go wrong! This has been termed the *Four-Cornered Contract,* developed by Julie Hay,[*] and it will help to clarify expectations across a range of communication channels. This tool can be used to explore who you need to have an agreement with and also if things have gone wrong—you can use it as a diagnostic tool to understand who you left out.

Take time to ensure that all those who are involved in the work understand and have input into the stakeholder and communications plans that impact them. It may take a little more time upfront but will certainly stop conflict and confusion from being the outcome further down the track.

3.3.2 Group Structures

Matrix Structures

Cross-functional teams that are highly empowered to make decisions, solve conflict, and work fast are difficult to sustain in a classic functional organizational structure. Matrix structures provide far more flexibility and opportunity for teams to work efficiently.

A matrix structure is normally depicted by two axes, with common labels such as "product" or "program of work/project" on one axis and "function" or "resource" on the other. Dimensions of both axes exercise defined levels of control over the tasks performed and the resources utilized.

The differences lie in the degree of emphasis on functional or program-of-work/project responsibility. The weak matrix is closer to a classic functional organization, whereas a balanced or strong matrix is closer to a pure team-based projectized organization. In all cases, the accountabilities and responsibilities must be clear, including the establishment of work governance models (e.g., steering committees, executive sponsors, etc.).

The following provides some key points on each type and a typical sample of one matrix type:

- **Weak Matrix.** In a weak matrix, program-of-work and/or project resources remain in their business units and report to the functional managers of each business unit. Progression of program-of-work and/or project activities is coordinated by a person(s) performing a coordinator function.

---

[*] Hay, 1995

Managing Groups—Working Together for Great Outcomes 81

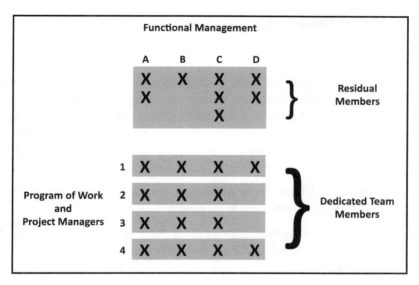

Figure 3.4 Strong Matrix

- **Balanced Matrix.** In a balanced matrix, program-of-work and/or project resources are seconded and report directly to program-of-work or project managers for the duration of each initiative.

- **Strong Matrix.** In the strong matrix (Fig. 3.4), program-of-work and/or project resources are dedicated and report directly to program-of-work and/or project managers on a daily basis. There is a much smaller group of business-as-usual resources that are dedicated to opex activity.

Projectized Structure

This form, a variation of the strong matrix, shows that all work is achieved through portfolio, programs of work, and projects. This clearly requires a portfolio-driven culture, in which the organization is seeking to better integrate its functions in order to reduce cost, gain efficiency, and maximize profits and competitiveness. In order to do this, many organizations look for guidance to move from a functional setup to a more projectized structure. A truly projectized organization operates without any specific functions—rather, it may have a series of portfolios run by cross-functional teams that have high levels of empowerment, accountability, and responsibility. This option, to be sustainable, requires the organization, and perhaps even the sector it operates within, to have mature, high levels of portfolio, program-of-work, and project management capability.

3.3.3 Group Dynamics

Influence

John Maxwell, in his excellent book *The 21 Irrefutable Laws of Leadership,*[*] stated that "The measure of leadership is influence—nothing more, nothing less."

We can think of influence as one's ability to persuade someone to do something for you as if it were their intention all along. This is conducted in an open, transparent, and trustful manner. To achieve this, we must exercise a series of four steps, as follows:

Step 1: Prepare. A leader must spend time crafting a plan on how to begin, develop, and achieve/conclude influence.

Step 2: Create connection. This needs to be a genuine desire to develop rapport (refer to Section 2.2 on page 38). Being sincere as well as vulnerable will assist greatly, as will the communications methods you use.

Step 3: Assess other person/group needs. This builds from the previous steps and adds the use of listening, clarifying, and reflecting engagement traits to establish what the other person's needs are. Some will be similar, and others will be varied and different. Catering for the majority should be the first response action, followed by engagement with others on the risk zone of the continuum of commitment, where individuals could "lurch" from a position of support to a position of being negative.

Step 4: Be persuasive. Use repeating, reinforcing, re-aligning, and supporting actions to build trust via a consistent communication mechanism that persuades others to follow, adopt, or act depending on the situation and outcome you wish to achieve.

Influence is planned in terms of consideration—it is sincere, and it is compassionate. It is certainly not about office politics or unwritten ground rules. Every leader, including Sam, needs to have a high degree of influencing capability to be successful. This is more than any claim to power an organizational job position might offer.

The Act of Leading

Earlier in this section, we discussed the great and still relevant work of Tuckman/Jensen[†] in terms of understanding group dynamics. In addition to that, we

---

[*] Maxwell, 2007
[†] Tuckman and Jensen, 1977

Managing Groups—Working Together for Great Outcomes 83

need to add specific factors such as leadership practice, high performance, and influence.

As we discussed in Section 1, good leadership practice starts with setting the example ourselves. Sharing and communicating a desired vision of the way forward is essential and can be strengthened further by influencing and empowering others to build a genuine culture of community. In turn, this will foster a level of high performance that is triggered by the common purpose (shared vision) and fueled by the encouragement of debate, problem-solving energy, treating mistakes as opportunities, and roles shared to accomplish output via individual and team talent. If done on a constant and consistent basis, everybody gets involved and feels as though their contribution is recognized and celebrated as appropriate. Be truthful and consistent in the use of your leadership principles, your styles, and your techniques.

More on Thinking Style Preferences

In Section 1, we discussed the quadrant perspective of the Herrmann International Group's thinking style preferences* in order to understanding another person. Here we scale that to a wider team or group perspective. As a team or group leader, you should strive to get a balance of thinking preferences into each team to allow those teams to quickly combat the challenges posed by the VUCA world and your organization's reaction to it, where nimbleness and speed of delivery will be essential. A simple yet effective gauge of differences in thinking styles can be gained by asking yourself these questions:

- Why do some groups work well together and others do not?

- Why are some groups productive and fun to work with and others are unproductive and boring?

- Why can the same person do extremely well in one group and poorly in another?

Knowing thinking preferences in advance can provide a leader with opportunities to swap people around different teams or groups in order to achieve a better balance. Done well, using a thinking style radar chart, this sets the team on the path of consistent high performance. This adds real value to decision making, problem solving, conflict resolution, and—perhaps most important—team and group dynamics. It should also be a core part of any team agreement.

As shown in Figure 3.5, the quadrant perspectives are Analytic and Organized on the left side, and Integrating and Interpersonal on the right side. Typically,

---

* Herrmann International Group, n.d.

84   The Business of People: Leadership for the Changing World

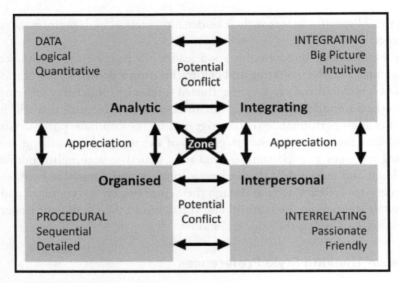

Figure 3.5   Quadrant Perspectives

an appreciation exists between the analytic and organized thinkers and between those who have interpersonal or integrating preferences. Conversely, there is potential conflict between those who have an analytic preference and those who have an integrating preference, as well as the potential for conflict between those with an organized preference and those with an interpersonal preference.

A series of easy-to-use tools provides a leader and his/her team with pragmatic and robust systems that enhance overall performance. These can be applied to an individual, team, or group (see Tool S3.2 on page 101).

Drama and Winners' Triangles

The Drama Triangle is a model developed by Stephen Karpman back in 1968[*] to assist people to be more mindful and impactful in their interactions (see Fig. 3.6). The model suggests three habitual roles which people often unconsciously take:

- Victim
- Persecutor
- Rescuer

---

[*] Karpman 1968

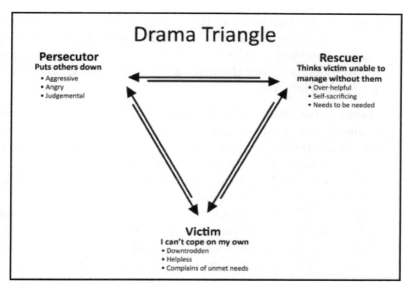

Figure 3.6 Drama Triangle

The key to understanding this model is that all three positions avoid taking responsibility for self. Instead we expect others to change or to do something.

It is called a Drama Triangle because we can move quickly between all three positions, exchanging positions with others and all the while not taking responsibility for ourselves.

For example, the victim could turn on the rescuer, or the rescuer switches to persecuting.

The apex of the triangle is blame.

- **Victim.** The role of Victim is probably the most familiar. Here, we hold anyone and anything but ourselves responsible for solving our problems. As Victim, we are likely to attract the attention of someone willing to take the Rescuer position.

- **Rescuer.** In the Rescuer role, we take over responsibility for the other person, do things on their behalf without consulting them; but, as with the Victim role, the Rescuer does not take responsibility for themselves either. As the Rescuer, the response can be anger at the lack of appreciation or response of the Victim, and so this can shift into the position of Persecutor. The Victim can also easily shift into Persecutor position, angry at the way others will not take away their problems, or even angry at the way they do.

- **Persecutor.** The third position, Persecutor, acts by punishing and blaming others. In the persecutor role, we accuse others. We are unwilling to negotiate or problem solve, and we can be abusive. We place all responsibility for issues on anyone else that we can blame. The Victim is an easy target for the Persecutor.

The dynamic in the Drama Triangle is such that the Persecutor can rapidly flip into Victim, Victim into Persecutor, Rescuer into Victim, etc. Each position is equally accessible (and at great speed) to any of us while we refuse to take responsibility for ourselves in relating to another person.

While the drama triangle explains what is occurring, it does not help us to get out of the drama. However, the Winners' Triangle, discussed by Acey Choy in 1990,* does. The Winners' Triangle (see Fig. 3.7) offers a choice to interact differently, by being mindful of yourself. Taking responsibility for self is the essential shift between the dynamics of the Drama Triangle and those of the Winners' Triangle. Here the apex of the triangle is self-responsibility.

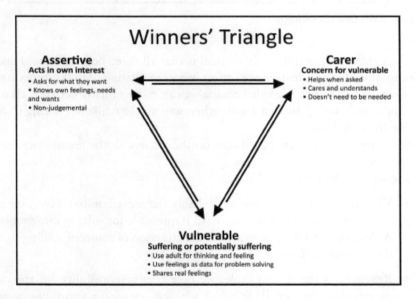

Figure 3.7 Winners' Triangle

Easy to label as simply taking responsibility for oneself, it is often much harder to actually do. The three positions in the Winners' Triangle correspond

---
* Choy, 1990

Managing Groups—Working Together for Great Outcomes 87

directly to those in the Drama Triangle. By taking responsibility for self, we can no longer remain in the Persecutor position.

- **Assertive.** We move to Assertive, no longer looking to blame others or to punish them. The Assertive person is clear about their own needs and boundaries but is also open to those of others, which enables them to negotiate.

- **Carer.** In the same way as Persecutor corresponds to Assertive, so Rescuer corresponds to the Carer position. Behaving as Carer, one neither abdicates one's own needs nor over-commits. The Carer dissolves the illusion that one can take another's problem from them and solve it for them, without diminishing or disempowering them.

  Whatever commitment the Carer makes can be relied on, and is given fully, without pulling back again. If they cannot fulfil their commitment, they are accountable. They are sensitive to the other person's experience and needs—not least their right and need to be responsible for themselves.

- **Vulnerable.** The converse to Victim is Vulnerable. To be Vulnerable conjures up being weak, exposed to potential abuse and disempowerment. It is something we often learn instinctively to avoid or hide, not only from others, but also from ourselves. Attempts to avoid experiencing our vulnerability are, however, likely to result in the powerlessness, disempowerment, or abusiveness of the Victim, Rescuer, or Persecutor.

  When we are vulnerable, taking responsibility for ourselves may take the form of admitting that we cannot manage, and asking for the help we need. However, we do not assume someone else has to help us, nor do we resent them if they choose not to. The thought of experiencing our vulnerability can be scary, even frightening.

  Paradoxically, the actual experience can lead to unexpected empowerment. There is real power in being vulnerable, because we are able to acknowledge the reality of the situation we are facing and work on solving the real problem.

3.3.4 Power Within a Group

Every group of people, no matter what the size or purpose, has at least one power dynamic at work. In most cases this is quite normal, as long as cultural norms and team agreements are not breached. As a leader, you need to be aware that there are a number of ways people can claim, develop, or exercise power. We feel

88 The Business of People: Leadership for the Changing World

that the work done by John French and Bertram Raven on Social Power[*] is as good a guide as any. They developed the following classifications:

- **Reward power.** The ability to reward team members in whatever way appropriate. Usually has positive outcomes although can suffer from scalability aspects.

- **Formal power.** Sometimes referred to as *legitimate power*. Formal positioning together with authority and the right to give direction.

- **Referent power.** Admiration of leader resulting in trust and desire to follow. Leader becomes a role model.

- **Expert power.** Function of the knowledge, skills, and experience of the leader that people respect and will follow.

- **Informational power.** Uses the possession of specific information or data as a power base. Usually has a short-term impact.

- **Penalty power.** Sometimes referred to as *coercive power*. The ability to punish, resulting in negative outcomes for the recipient. Forces people to work in a certain way.

And lastly, we have added the concept of

- **Relational power.** The power that you have from forming strong relationships with people, regardless of their other forms of power.

It is not to say that one style is right and another is wrong, albeit some are more desirable than others. Situations will dictate. However, as a leader you may want to think about the two types of power you can exert. These are:

- **Power over.** This style has an attitude towards wielding power over others. A person using this kind of power can reward and punish, meet or not meet others' needs, create obedience. People receiving this power type will generally fight back, flee or avoid, shut down or obey. People who are regularly punished will avoid contact with those whom they see as the punishers.

- **Power with.** This style has an attitude towards collaborative power aiming to work together to be powerful. A person using this power can create value and develop options, enhance both parties' concerns, find creative solutions. People receiving this power type will generally join with you

---

[*] Raven and French, 1959

and show loyalty. People who are rewarded often will work hard to emulate the same behaviors again.

3.3.5 Dealing with Conflict

Recognition of Conflict

Although often thought of as negative, conflict can in fact be a positive experience, in that its resolution can lead to improvements in team harmony, in hierarchical structures, in peer relationships, and in organizational performance. Conflict can appear to be, and often is, complex; however, it often arises from one or more of these common sources:

- Conflict of style. Triggered by differences in learning or thinking preferences or even working style and practices.

- Conflict of opinion or fact. Triggered using casual or anecdotal information that is not validated with data.

- Conflict of values. Triggered by a range of aspects including culture, personal theme and values, degree of professionalism.

- Conflict of needs/goals. Triggered by misaligned expectations that may or may not relate to overindulgence.

In terms of assessing and recognizing which type of conflict might exist in a group or department, Table 3.2 will assist you.

Table 3.2 Positive versus Negative Conflict Recognition

Positive (Managed) Conflict	Negative (Out-of-Control) Conflict
Strengthens relationships and builds teamwork.	Damages relationships and discourages cooperation.
Encourages open communication and cooperative problem solving.	Results in defensiveness and hidden agendas.
Resolves disagreements quickly and increases productivity.	Wastes time, money, and human energy.
Deals with real issues and concentrates on collaborative resolution.	Focuses on fault finding and blame.
Makes allies and diffuses anger.	Creates emotions and enemies.
Airs all sides of an issue in a positive, supportive environment.	Is frustrating, stress producing, and energy draining.
Is calm and focused toward results.	Is often loud, hostile, and chaotic.

90 The Business of People: Leadership for the Changing World

Each of those sources has constructive ways of resolving the conflict so that people are able to express and work through their differences without the risk of, or necessity to, damage one another and slow the organization. To effectively and constructively manage conflict, there are skills, guidelines, and considerations that can be used to good effect. These are covered in the following sections.

Resolution Techniques

The best way to manage destructive conflict is to prevent it from happening in the first place by using the concepts and ideas we have discussed previously, especially a well-thought-through Team Agreement. However, if you find yourself in a conflict resolution situation, there is still much you can do in the moment.

Before resolution can occur, two things need to happen: first, a good enough understanding of the causes of the conflict and its history; and second, a willingness for the parties to work together to find a resolution.

Often parties will be very clear about how they see things and how the other party sees it differently. That is to be expected. If they agreed, there wouldn't be the conflict. Conflict is not about the fight; the purpose of conflict is to have the other party recognize or take account of a concern that currently they perceive is not occurring and take steps to resolve that concern.

All require skill and commitment to resolution. If you are not the right person for the job, do not enter this realm, as you will make things worse.

In terms of preparing for conflict resolution, your initial consideration should be given to:

- What is actually the issue? Substantive, relationship, or process?

- What is the source?

- Have we experienced similar conflict in the past?

- What is the level of commitment by the parties involved?

- What else is happening currently?

Next is to turn your attention to skills. Make sure that the person(s) tasked with solving the conflict has skills that include the following:

- Skill to initiate discussion—choose the issue(s) you want to address and be specific.

- Skill to communicate—choose micro-communications methods and language that is concise and that avoids vague or general terms.

- Skill to effectively listen.

Managing Groups—Working Together for Great Outcomes 91

- Skill to recognize the need and ability to make personal changes—be clear about what you want to change and follow through.
- Skill to learn and use what you have learned.
- Skill to seek out resources as necessary.

To solve conflict, the following guideline can be adopted or adapted:

- Have a plan and a back-up plan.
- Attack the problem, not the person(s).
- Be clear about what you see, how you judge, and how you react to people and situations.
- Verbalize your feelings appropriately.
- Understand and take charge of your own feelings and behaviors.
- Move from justification to resolution.
- Look forward (opportunity), not backward (blaming).
- Analyze the situation and view it from both sides.
- Recognize how you may have contributed to the situation.
- Identify the points about which you can compromise rather than demand.
- Be open and make every effort to respond in a positive manner.
- Seek independent expertise if the parties' skills are not adequate or focus is required elsewhere.

Specific activities in a group setting might include:

- Manage your own emotions and remain in your adult self.
- Ask the parties to step out of the substantive discussion you are having and reflect on how you are working together. Compare against the Team Agreement.
- Use a two-step check-in with the group. Ask how the group is working together; if there is no acknowledgement of the conflict publicly, check in with individuals by going into a paired discussion and then seek feedback.
- Once the concern is articulated, do the work to resolve the conflict or acknowledge and put aside for now, depending on the group's decision.
- Develop a process agreement for a way forward, if not already in the Team Agreement.

- Go back into the substantive discussion.
- Maintain an unconditionally constructive attitude.
- Use the Circle Process Tool (see Tool S3.1, page 100).

Using a Conflict Mode Instrument

Understanding your own and others' conflict style gives you great power to reflect on the conflict and the dynamic. We have used the following instrument for many years.

The Thomas-Kilmann Conflict Mode Instrument (TKI)* was designed to measure a person's behavior in conflict situations. TKI conflict situations are those in which the concerns of two people appear to be incompatible. In such situations, we can describe an individual's behavior along two dimensions: (1) assertiveness (i.e., the extent to which the person attempts to satisfy his/her own concerns), and (2) cooperativeness (i.e., the extent to which the person attempts to satisfy the other persons' concerns). Figure 3.8 shows the instrument model.

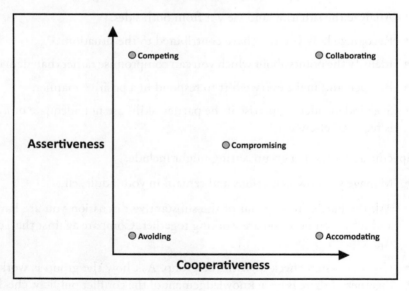

Figure 3.8 Thomas-Kilmann Conflict Mode Instrument Model. (*Source:* © 2009–2019 by Kilmann Diagnostics. All rights reserved. Original figure is available at: http://www.kilmanndiagnostics.com/overview-thomas-kilmann-conflict-mode-instrument-tki)

---

* Thomas and Kilmann, n.d.

These two basic dimensions of behavior define five different modes of responding to conflict situations:

1. **Competing** is assertive and uncooperative—an individual pursues his/her own concerns at the other person's expense. This is a power-oriented mode in which you use whatever power seems appropriate to win your own position—your ability to argue, your rank, your economic sanctions. Competing means standing up for your rights, defending a position which you believe is correct, or simply trying to win.

2. **Accommodating** is unassertive and cooperative—the complete opposite of competing. When accommodating, the individual neglects his own concerns to satisfy the concerns of the other person; there is an element of self-sacrifice in this mode. Accommodating might take the form of self-less generosity or charity, obeying another person's order when you would prefer not to, or yielding to another's point of view.

3. **Avoiding** is unassertive and uncooperative—the person pursues neither his own concerns nor those of the other individual. Thus he does not deal with the conflict. Avoiding might take the form of diplomatically sidestepping an issue, postponing an issue until a better time, or simply withdrawing from a threatening situation.

4. **Compromising** is moderate in both assertiveness and cooperativeness. The objective is to find some expedient, mutually acceptable solution that partially satisfies both parties. It falls between competing and accommodating. Compromising gives up more than competing but less than accommodating. Likewise, it addresses an issue more directly than avoiding, but does not explore it in as much depth as collaborating. In some situations, compromising might mean splitting the difference between the two positions, exchanging concessions, or seeking a quick middle-ground solution.

5. **Collaborating** is both assertive and cooperative—the complete opposite of avoiding. Collaborating involves an attempt to work with others to find some solution that fully satisfies both parties' concerns. It means digging into an issue to pinpoint the underlying needs and wants of the two individuals. Collaborating between two persons might take the form of exploring a disagreement to gain insights from each other or trying to find a creative solution to an interpersonal problem.

Each of us is capable of using all five conflict-handling modes. None of us can be characterized as having a single style in reacting to or dealing with

94 The Business of People: Leadership for the Changing World

conflict. But certain people use some modes better than others and, therefore, tend to rely on those modes more heavily than others—whether because of temperament or practice.

Using Independent Expertise

If after a reasonable period of time the parties to a conflict cannot resolve, then seeking expertise is the next logical step. This can take many forms, but a recognized approach is an alternative dispute resolution path. This uses independent people and can follow an escalation, mediation, arbitration, or legislation option(s). Other than escalation, these options are usually provided by external parties. However, each has different levels of resolution and follows different routes. The key to success is to build a connection between the parties and brief the parties in a similar manner, taking care to avoid connectors that present a non-factual opinion. Once the connection and briefing are established, the leader needs to step back and trust the parties to progress and resolve the situation appropriately between them.

Occasionally, escalation or mediation will not resolve the situation, and then arbitration is the next logical step. At this stage the parties are committing to a decision that is made on the conflict by others. This is also the same for a legislative approach, in which a court will determine a resolution that the parties are obligated to accept.

3.3.6 Managing Group Processes

Being able to manage group processes and lead groups in the moment is a powerful set of skills. If you feel you are not that sort of a leader, you will need to be able to see that in others and ask them to take the role of the facilitator in a group situation.

We have all attended meetings and group occasions in which the leader was not the right person for the job. So, either upskill or create the space and delegate that role to someone who can do the job well. Both Iain and Madeleine have seen many group situations in which the leader has asked someone else to facilitate the proceedings. This does not take away from the leader's accountability or role responsibility.

In any group there are three types of leadership roles that you, as the leader, need to be aware of[*]:

---

[*] Clarke, Dawson, and Bredehoft, 2014

- **Responsible leader.** The person who people go to when problems occur or when people outside the group want to talk to the boss.

- **Effective leader.** The person who makes sure that stuff gets done.

- **Psychological leader.** The person who creates the emotional and trust level in the group—he or she who must be obeyed!

It could be that they are all the same person, or that different people take up these roles. Scan the groups you lead—at work or in community—and see if you can spot who takes which leadership role in each setting. Mostly these roles happen without any overt discussion or awareness of the group. Conflict can occur when there is a difference of opinion about who has what leadership role. Usually the conflict will not be about the "power" or relationship or leadership dynamic. It will be played out in a discussion about substance. Frequently, this will mean that the conversation will not resolve the issue. So, get out of the substance and talk about the relationship and process. You will make a lot more progress that way.

As the leader, you are responsible for ensuring that you have the correct person in each of these roles to achieve the purpose of your team, group, or organization. When you are the leader of the group, be aware of the roles, play to your strengths, and intervene if the people in the roles are not contributing appropriately to the agreement and purpose of the group.

Facilitation

Facilitation is the ability to make the work of a group easy—to help the group do its job, whatever that task is. As the leader, you are the primary facilitator and therefore primarily concerned with how the group is working together as well as the substance of that work. As a leader, of course, you are also deeply committed to producing the expected output/outcome. But to help the group work well, the facilitation must be ego free. Here a decision must be made for the good of the output/outcome. Ask yourself if you are the best person to be in the facilitators' role, and if not, then delegate and give a team member an opportunity to lead.

Good facilitators understand the life cycle of groups, can diagnose what stage a group is at, and know the thinking and learning preferences of that group. They know how to prepare for a facilitation session by using a range of communication skills and tools and can utilize purposeful facilitation techniques for different situations. How is it possible to do all this at once? First (of course) it will start with you!

96 The Business of People: Leadership for the Changing World

According to Dale Hunter,[*] an expert in facilitation, before you can think of facilitating groups, you need to think about facilitating yourself. This is about growing, developing, and training yourself to be aware of how you are and what you are responding to in the moment. Some questions to get you thinking:

- Are you feeling easy with yourself the way you are right now?
- Are you relaxed with your body?
- Are you serene with your feelings?
- Are you relaxed with your thoughts?
- Are you easy with your gender and sexual orientation?
- Are you satisfied with your cultural and national affinities?
- Are you comfortable being you?

If you notice a hesitation as you ran through these questions, then do explore your response, because that may be a signpost to build on your self-awareness.

Being a facilitator is a tough gig—your lack of self-awareness could make or break a project.

How you as the facilitator respond to a challenge or to negative feedback, or your failure to recognize a situation, can make the work of the group so much harder. There are three aspects you may need to grow:

- Self-awareness
- Self-reflecting
- Self-accepting

Initially, this involves recognizing and understanding your triggers, growing, developing, and training yourself, and being able to say, "I accept myself completely—warts and all." Secondly, it involves the building of trust and relationship which we have talked about using the Tuckman/Jensen framework[†] and Herrmann models.[‡] Thirdly, a good facilitator plans the event, including having all the administration thought through, then designs the group work time with the outcome and learning/thinking/conflict/working styles in mind. For any facilitation session, you may want to develop a run sheet (see Tool S3.4 on page 102).

- **Planning.** Most facilitation requires a lot of pre-organization. It pays for you as the facilitator to ensure that these basic matters are covered

---

[*] Hunter et al., 2007

[†] Tuckman and Jensen, 1977

[‡] Herrmann, n.d.

Managing Groups—Working Together for Great Outcomes 97

because it will be you in front of the group looking silly if that work has not been done. From booking venues, ensuring the space is adequate, has the correct equipment, inviting attendees, having materials and refreshments are available.

- **Designing the facilitation process.** Start with the outcome in mind. Look at the amount of time you have. Think of the procedures you will use to build trust; you need to begin with connecting people as human beings, providing structure to allow safety to develop before people can get down to work. Ensure you have time enough for the closing session. Less experienced facilitators will often run out of time at the end of the day and not get to the "commitment to action" part. There is no gold in doing anything that means people are unclear about who is doing what, when, and how. You will often find that people want to do too much and therefore end up failing. Expect to push back in the planning stages to give yourself and the group the time and space to do the work.

Team Coaching

In Section 2, we discussed the differences between coaching and mentoring. We touched on benefits that can be captured from one-on-one coaching and one-on-one mentoring. The notion of team coaching in the workplace is not as commonplace as it is for individuals. However, we consider that team coaching, not unlike what we see in a sports team, can create sustainable high performance. Challenges exist, however, and a clear, thought-out plan together with good execution are the keys to success. It is likely that the plan will include sub-coaches, which allows larger teams to be coached, with the sub-coaches concentrating on specific aspects of the plan.

While Sam has enjoyed success with coaching and mentoring in his EPMO role, the challenge now is to scale up for the whole department. Sam requires several sub-coaches and will seek those from outside the organization. Sam also considers that a variation on a team agreement that was used successfully with the EPMO team would be a great place to start.

There are also some additional ways that you can consider supporting and encouraging your teams.

Team Supervision

Supervision is a process in which the team supervisor enables, guides, and facilitates the team members in meeting certain organisational, professional, and personal objectives. These objectives are professional competence, accountable and safe practice, continuing professional development, education, and support.

98 The Business of People: Leadership for the Changing World

In a team supervision setting, the group will generally meet for one and a half hours about every six weeks to discuss matters concerning the team members. It is a confidential and safe time for members to recognise their team vulnerabilities and work to problem solve them.

The benefits of team supervision are:

- Problem solving

- Resilience building

- Enhanced accountability

- Increased feeling of support

- Development of professional skills, improved efficiency

- Decreased feelings of isolation and role ambiguity

A typical agenda might be:

- Welcome

- Agreements

- Round—what has gone well, what is my challenge

- Identify topics and work on them by asking questions and having people think about possibilities

- Reflection round

- Closing

Action Learning Sessions

This is a facilitated discussion in which one member of the team identifies a concern and is in the "hot seat" for perhaps 30 minutes.

An action learning session works by having one person describing the problem, then group members can only ask questions. The rule continues that you can only make a statement if you have been asked a question. You might have an external facilitator or appoint one from the team. The facilitator and the group will help keep everyone on track.

The benefits of an action learning group are, according to Dearlove[*]:

- It is efficient because it uses a genuine problem or issue as a learning vehicle.

---

[*] Dearlove, 2003

Managing Groups—Working Together for Great Outcomes 99

- It takes a group approach.
- It accepts or assumes there are no "experts" (naïve questions illuminate issues).
- It focuses on asking questions rather than providing solutions.
- It reduces time between learning and application.
- It concentrates attention on results and process.
- It focuses on the present and future.
- It provides feedback.
- It discovers innovative solutions.
- It increases organisational commitment.
- It enhances organisational learning.

Team Away Sessions

Taking time out to refine the work of the team, to refocus values and behavior, is all part and parcel of the work of the team. This will then align the team through the team agreement or charter. Being an efficient and competent team requires a maintenance program. Taking care of your culture will help you to do this.

Focus the team away sessions on the purpose and objective of the group. Doing fun activities for fun's sake is nice, but not if that activity does not build the relationship within the team or develop deeper awareness of self or others.

Regular Team Meetings

Always be clear about the purpose of the team meetings. For example, do they aim to share information about the content of the team's work? Perhaps to pass on information from the wider organization? Are they to support each of the team members, or to share new learning and opportunities?

Many leaders and team members consider their meetings to be a waste of time. As a leader, you have a great opportunity to inspire and encourage your team through the way the team meetings are conducted. Refer to the content of Team Agreements on page 76 and Tool S3.3 on page 101 for an example.

3.4 Case Study

Sam reflects on a particular leadership situation a colleague had experienced in another large organization. His colleague's department had launched a project

100   The Business of People: Leadership for the Changing World

to upgrade an IT system using internal staff supplemented with a few external contractors. The project was for a straight-forward hardware and software upgrade to a business system the department relied upon. A budget value of $5.2 million was approved and a team of 15 people with various skill sets gathered.

The sponsor was a departmental line manager who had appointed the project manager. Unfortunately, the project manager was inadequate at leading people and spent most of his time building a very large activity schedule for the scope of work. The team were leaderless. The team also had some very strong personalities that were causing constantly shifting priorities. Soon the project manager resigned and a second project manager, followed by a third, were appointed to replace further resignations.

When the fourth project manager was appointed, Sams' colleague knew the investment was in trouble and unlikely to deliver any value. The situation was validated when an independent review revealed that the team were in disarray, the budget was being consumed, but little physical progress was evident. The large activity schedule was ineffective and was constantly being reworked by the fourth project manager. The sponsor had made all the project manager appointments.

Turnaround actions that followed the review included appointing a professional project manager (the others were not!), scrapping the huge activity schedule, and changing some of the team members for better balance. It also included the appointment of a new, experienced sponsor who would be supportive in the turnaround actions.

From this reflection, Sam knew that group dynamics was hugely important to his business desires and the departmental objectives.

3.5 Tools

Tool S3.1: Circle Process*

This is a restorative process and has a clear step-wise process to follow if you are going to use a circle. To ensure the best possible chance for it to work well and resolve difficult issues, follow these carefully and have a skilled facilitator lead the circle. The guide provides detailed information for the steps below.

- Welcome

- Opening

---

* Pranis, 2017b

Managing Groups—Working Together for Great Outcomes   101

- Explain centerpiece
- Explain talking piece
- Purpose of the circle
- Introduction/check-in round
- Values/guidelines
- Storytelling round
- Exploring issues
- Agreement
- Clarify expectations
- Check-out round
- Thanks

Remember, it can often be useful to have someone from outside the group facilitate these interventions. You will make it worse if you do not do it soon enough or do not have the skills to facilitate.

Tool S3.2: Diversity Game

The powerful yet fun card game that explores thinking style preferences. Available from Applied Creativity Inc. in Florida, USA.

Tool S3.3: Example Team Agreement/Charter

We will:

- Keep our commitments to each other and openly communicate if there is a problem.
- Respect each other's opinion by listening carefully and asking questions.
- Decide when we have a problem which tool we will use to work through the concern.
- Take the time to share our knowledge and experiences when we think they might support the work of the team.
- Share the time in our team meetings.
- Start and finish on time.

102 The Business of People: Leadership for the Changing World

- Have an agenda.
- Leave our cell phones outside the meeting space.
- Clarify how a decision will be made.
- Have fun.
- Go for an ice cream/coffee/walk together once a week.

Include outcome objective, coat of arms, group thinking styles, group learning styles, conflict resolution, decision making, etc.

Tool S3.4: Kick-Off Meeting Run Sheet

The use of this tool assists in creating a well-functioning and engaged team of people. Attendance should be from all core team members as well as key stakeholders. This ensures that they will know why they are there, how to engage, and what is required next.

The tool and content can be adapted for routine meetings that are held post kick-off.

Time	Activity	Resources
Prior to meeting	Book room—allow enough time to set up and tidy up. Prepare agenda. Send out invites. Organize refreshments.	People to assist if needed
15 mins. before first person might arrive	Time alone in the room to ensure you are in the right frame of mind, the room is clear of others, we have the equipment we need, in order to do the work.	Time, yourself
As people arrive	Greet people as they arrive, smile, shake hands, build rapport, encourage people to engage with each other as they arrive.	Flip chart, white board, pens, etc.
As required	Introductions: Name, role, who their substitute will be. Something about how they like to work—e.g., values, thinking styles, learning styles. What excites them about this work? Laptops, phones, gadgets off.	

continues on next page

Time	Activity	Resources
As required	Conduct ice breaker activity. Overview of objectives and parameters. Set up parking lot. Set up issues list. Review charter. Create/review team agreement. Identify early issues. Open discussion on way forward. Summarizes as necessary.	Laptop, data projector, etc.
Towards end	Review parking lot. Review issues list.	
10 mins.	Agree and document action points. Key messages for communication. Confirm next meeting.	Meeting minutes
10 mins.	Meeting review (how did the meeting go?)	
5 mins.	Close meeting.	

Tool S3.5: Facilitation Processes

- **Talking piece.** This is a process that can help in situations in which emotions are heightened, and people need to listen carefully to each other. A talking piece is an object that is passed around (we suggest that you choose something that has significance to the group). The rule is that the person holding the talking piece is the only one allowed to speak. People who are not holding the piece listen carefully and do not respond at that time.

- **Problem Solving Circle (PSC).** In a PSC the idea is to have people offer their best suggestion to a problem. It is not the same as brainstorming, where people throw up random and creative ideas that may not directly connect to the concern. It is an efficient and effective way of identifying options. Preparing for a PSC, the facilitator outlines the process:

  o The person who has identified (PI) the problem gives a two-minute situation scene-setting presentation.

  o They then, in one sentence, name the problem.

  o Everyone thinks carefully about what they consider their best suggestion—keeping within the values of the group.

104 The Business of People: Leadership for the Changing World

o The facilitator requests two people to record alternative suggestions.

o The team goes quickly round the group as each participant offers their one-sentence suggestion.

o The PI listens carefully and at the end of the suggestion looks at the person who gave the suggestion and says, "Thank you."

o People have the right to pass if they cannot think of a suggestion—the PI again says, "Thank you." At the end, those who passed are asked if they want to provide their idea.

o At the end the facilitator will say, "Take these suggestions and, away from the group, decide which of these are right for you in this situation."

The PSC will give everyone the opportunity to offer ideas, and so many problems can be put through the process in a short period of time. A PSC should take about five minutes if you include the two minutes outlining the context minutes.

Thanks to Jean Illsley Clarke for her Suggestion Circle, from which this idea was developed.[*]

Tool S3.6: Problem-Solving and Decision-Making Tools

We believe that the tools offered in the *Memory Jogger* book[†] provide a wide selection of micro-tools to teams for problem solving and decision-making. Examples of these are brainstorming, affinity diagrams, cost benefit analysis, and decision matrix.

---

[*] Clarke, 2014
[†] Goal QPC, n.d.

Section Four

Leading the Organization— Creating a Dynamic Organization Which Delivers Ongoing Value

Management is about doing things right.
Leadership is about doing the right things.

— Peter Drucker

4.1 The Story So Far—Building Organizational Competence

Sam is sitting in a Board of Directors meeting as the recently appointed CEO of the organization. The chair has introduced a discussion on combatting the VUCA world. The Board is uneasy about the ability of the organization to prepare and respond to the impacts of volatility, uncertainty, complexity, and ambiguity. To their credit, they realize that the VUCA world is more than just the impact from technological advancements.

106 The Business of People: Leadership for the Changing World

Prior to the meeting, Sam had been reflecting and recognized that today increasing numbers of organizational leaders are insisting that portfolio, program-of-work, and project management (P3M) techniques be used to ensure efficient achievement of organizational goals and business objectives. It is a universal trend and is seen across sectors in both the non-profit and for-profit environments globally. In terms of economic climates, portfolio management, which includes program-of-work and project management, is important because it delivers value in both buoyant and downturn times in which adaptability, time to market, efficient use of available funds, and people working well together are the keys to success. Sam is not surprised then that the rise of portfolio and program-of-work management is increasing rapidly as organizations take a more holistic view in terms of value creation and capture across both operational and capital expenditure. There are three critical factors that contribute to the ongoing success of organizations, and Sam now has the knowledge and skills to lay a foundation for consistent success. The critical factors are:

1. Organizational capability and maturity in doing business

2. Capability and skills of people in the organization

3. The need to simplify and be as adaptable as possible

Sam needs to convey those success factors to the Board members as well as to his direct reports.

Sam regards the capability and maturity factor as requiring the organization to be fully aware of its macro environment in terms of culture and purpose, business philosophy and ethics, and capability to perform and deliver efficiently and consistently any initiative from commencement through to completion and value capture. Making sure that existing skillsets are known and mapped to initiative type and scale is vital, as are the methods used to execute each initiative. Maturity also requires robust and appropriate P3M governance to be evident and in use. This would include leadership and ownership, organizational structure, commercial approaches, and decision making, plus macro change control. No initiative should commence without a business case that clearly demonstrates both the output and the outcome (business value) and the alignment to one or more business objectives.

In relation to the second critical factor, Sam wants to invest in people development that is beyond the restriction of budget-controlled discretionary training amounts that are so commonplace, and hence considers that disparate line management and HR views often lead to money being squandered on personalized training that has questionable overall impact. Instead, personal development needs to be skill and knowledge based, part of a defined career path

Leading the Organization—Creating a Dynamic Organization 107

roadmap, and contribute directly to the vision and purpose of the organization. Being part of the organizational culture would be great!

The third factor is about agility, change, and speed. Organizations will need to challenge and likely change their current business models to create new ways of working that readily accept change, that simplify the way business is done, and that empower, and thereby trust, people further—all this in an environment that is cognizant of the health and safety of all people in the employment of the organization.

Looking toward the future, Sam wants to see more use of aligned portfolio, program-of-work, and project management techniques. These will underpin modern value management frameworks to support established project management and operational methods. However, in order to continue to reduce the risk of failure of complex initiatives, Sam realizes that phased approaches and associated dialogue be crystal clear on where each proposed initiative fits into the organization's business objectives. As the focus on the above critical factors continues, Sam will need to encourage the use of more incentive-based agreements that motivate toward a culture of success across each supply chain, for mutual benefit rather than the "us and them" approaches so often utilized today. Sam recognizes that help is needed and decides to enlist a personal mentor to reduce the isolation felt from time to time as well as to provoke deep thinking.

Sam recognizes that in order to lead the organization into the future, the focus must be on specific organizational competencies outlined in Section 4.3, Solutions of the Situation, below, in order to create an organization that is simplified yet robust, adaptable yet focused, fast yet careful. This will likely require periods of change to counter the effects of the VUCA world's impact the organization. Sam feels ready for this.

4.2 Case Study

Following the considerable building and infrastructure damage from the major earthquakes in Christchurch, New Zealand, businesses there have had a major focus on risk. This has followed a sustainability path using cloud-based technologies together with encouraging and supporting people to work remotely. To be able to lead organizations through this time required considerable people skills and large amounts of adaptability. Not all went smoothly; as some organizations floundered, some leaders and workers did too. However, the ones that did well maintained a focus on their people and supported them to work through tough times. The best leaders exercised power with people and encouraged them to get things done via their implementation quotients.

4.3 Solutions for the Situation

4.3.1 The 3P's to Success—Being Clear About What You Are Doing

Any organization that wishes to be adaptive, nimble, and consistently successful on value creation and capture must have an integrated approach to doing business. This requires careful planning and passionate belief to be successfully implemented and for full benefits to be gained. The solution revolves around a simplified yet powerful model, introduced in Iain's book *The Business of Portfolio Management—Boosting Organizational Value,* called the 3P's to Success. This is wider than the common process-oriented aspects of some models but keeps the implementation pragmatic in order to drive and gain results faster via improvement. The elements of the 3P's to Success model are:

- **Purpose.** Crafting a clear organizational vision that is combined with a robust purpose statement, setting strategic goals together with defined policy relating to that strategy, determining related critical success factors (CSFs), business objectives, and linkages to P3M governance. There must be a strong focus on and a "bringing to life" of culture embedded in this element. These cultural elements would need to be triggered, owned, and actively supported by the highest levels of governance in the organization (e.g., Board of Directors and executive managers). The adoption of scenario planning and value management as overarching frameworks will drive a realistic strategy output that has a higher implementation relationship with across-the-organization portfolio management adoption and the translation of strategic intentions and objectives into aligned, actionable plans. No confusing mission statement, no confusion between goals and objectives, and no half-hearted approaches. This is how you get ahead.

- **People.** Building from the purpose statement and recognizing that it is the people connected to the organization that truly make the difference— recognizing that strong empowerment of people through a living culture and well-defined accountability and responsibility frameworks is critical for success. Also, skill development and experiential learning, such as in value management, will allow people to use their head, heart, and gut to make better decisions much more quickly than any process-centric method hopes to achieve. However, Sam's biggest challenges, and therefore risks, could be associated with a generation of future workers that display traits of overindulgence. Sam begins to think about the challenges associated with blending those individuals into high-performing teams. The bottom line is to trust, develop, and empower your people to ensure that your organization achieves a productivity lift that is sustainable and contributes directly to increased performance.

- **Performance.** Maintaining a focus on driving for results is key here. This would include a simplified system of organizational performance management for the review and guidance toward multiple success points via CSF trending, program-of-work key performance indicators (KPIs), and other supporting data, including feedback from people and the affirmation of value capture, aka business benefits, being realized post–program of work delivery. The balancing of operational expenditure (opex) with capital expenditure (capex) to produce an integrated business plan should also be included in this element.

The mechanism to deliver this type of model is via an organization-wide cultural change initiative. It is not, and should never be, via mundane process-driven change management approaches that, unfortunately, we see too often. We need more of what we term "passionate change" of all types that is integrated and operates in the same manner at all levels of the organization.

In the beginning of the "age of simplicity," we encourage you as a leader and reader of this book to find ways to utilize the 3P's to Success model in a manner that is simple to deploy and that becomes contagious as a result. Remember, people will follow you if they understand what is required and uncertainty is removed.

4.3.2 Culture—Delivering the Culture That Supports Your Vision

Every interaction you have as a leader will influence the organizational culture either positively or negatively. The discussion in Section 3 on the Tuckman/Jensen Model of Team Dynamics[*] can be considered as a form of cultural behavior; so too can the principles, styles, and techniques discussed in Section 2.

Expanding those to an organizational perspective puts a spotlight firmly on culture. This is certainly one element of organizational DNA that should be and can be improved upon. As we look toward the future, there are several interrelated areas that will require careful positioning so as to accommodate and blend the different generations of the 21st-century workplace.

---

[*] Tuckman and Jensen, 1977

Culture is, and must be advocated as, something that is more than a few selected words that have been grouped together by well-intentioned HR teams but that only act as a masquerade toward a cultural statement. It is also more than a bland statement that is talked about by some, ignored by the majority, and replaced with mid-management process layers.

Often, we see confusion between culture and climate within an organization, which further distorts the notion of a living, consistent, and sustainable culture. The desired and macro image of the organization's culture should focus around norms, values, and behaviors, whereas organizational climate is determined by micro perception, atmosphere, and the dreaded "unwritten ground rules." Organizational climate allows for the distortion, via opinions and perceptions of people, of the quality and characteristics of the desired culture. Clashes and confusion arise when the type of culture being pursued conflicts with the day-to-day climate. An example could be where a culture that is market oriented clashes with a climate that is rule and process oriented. The climate of an organization is likely to change frequently based on, for example, direct influence from senior leaders or via an external event. Organizational climate, therefore, is easier to experience and measure than organizational culture. The more consistency between the desired culture and the day-to-day climate interactions across the organization, the more the organization will flourish. It is our belief that all leaders need to understand the difference between culture and climate—and make sure that everybody in the organizations does also.

Here is an actual example: A large company in the manufacturing sector had one division that was performing very well, and the climate was consistent with the desired culture. Concerns were addressed when they were raised, and people were held accountable to the values. However, in another division, a fork-lift driver was known to "bump" into people he did not like, and the response from the leadership was that it would create too much drama to stop that behavior. Those pockets of inconsistency and the failure of leadership to address the serious issue were undermining the efforts of the whole organization.

Bringing people together in a culture that embraces the common vision and purpose for the future organization will be one of the greatest leadership challenges going forward into the VUCA world. In our view, two critical areas will influence the success level:

1. The need for ongoing flexibility and nimbleness toward change

2. Bringing together and developing groups of disparate people from various generations and traits such as overindulgence.

To develop a culture that will meet and compensate the above as well as one that is seen as genuine will require leaders to either correct, adapt, or develop a culture that includes the following attributes:

o Deep understanding of how the VUCA world is likely to impact the organization

o Well articulated vision statement that is supported by a clear purpose statement

o Well defined and well communicated set of true strategic goals that relate to the vision and purpose

o A set of integrated business objectives derived from the strategic goals

o Smart people that are fully empowered, united, and focused on their work endeavors

o A light approach to doing business which allows for the greatest amount of flexibility possible

o A focus on outcomes that considers value capture that is more than just a monetary perspective and which contributes to achievement of one or more business objectives

This list of seven attributes is fully consistent with the 3P's to Success model discussed earlier. Leaders must continually discuss, review, and—when required—adjust actions to make sure that commitment to culture is a continual and collaborative effort. Furthermore, leaders must show the way by identifying critical behaviors and then demonstrating and advocating for them continuously while encouraging others to adopt.

Culture is not a practice or set of policy rules that HR departments manage, nor is it a seemingly randomly selected group of buzz words that are populated around the workplace. Culture needs to be an agenda item of Board and executive meetings in which directors and managers take time to discuss whether clashes or confusion between culture and climate exist.

The culture that is developed via the above list of seven attributes and tested at all levels of the workplace will be the culture that is right for your organization.

But how do you do this? How can you influence and change the culture of an organization and monitor the climate of groups or teams? There are key concepts to understand how culture works. Some of these we have covered in the earlier sections.

112   The Business of People: Leadership for the Changing World

- **Organizational structure.** How the organization is set up to deal with the future

- **Recognition.** How people are recognized and rewarded, both as individuals and as teams

- **Power.** Leadership styles and the interchange of those throughout the organization

- **Psychological safety.** Comfort of belief and wellbeing associated with how people feel

- **Ethics.** Those internal and external professional standards

One way to help influence culture is to understand about recognition, which we mentioned briefly in Section 2. In the context of culture, recognition is a set of organizational "stroking" patterns.

A stroke is a unit of recognition; it can be positive or negative, conditional or unconditional, verbal or non-verbal. Eric Berne's book *The Games People Play* says that we are rewarded for any interaction—negative or positive. Being stroked gives recognition from one person to another and is essential to life.

It has been shown that babies need actual physical strokes in order to remain alive. Adults can get by on fewer physical strokes by getting verbal strokes instead; positive strokes such as praise or expressions of appreciation, or negative strokes such as judgments or "put downs." Each stroke lets people know they are alive.

Each person develops stroking patterns that match their needs. The impact of each stroke depends on how it is sent by the deliverer of the stroke and how it is taken by the receiver.

An organization will also develop its unique stroking pattern. Understanding this will help deliver the culture that you are aiming for. Often, we are unaware of the strokes we are giving and therefore cannot understand why certain behaviors continue. What we pay attention to—consciously or not—will be where the emphasis is placed.

As we know from Section 1, organizations have their own scripts (Organizational Transactional Analysis [TA]) that may have been carried from the organization's forebears. The recognition patterns in the organization will mirror the life script of these forebears.

Individual examples:

- **Positive Conditional.** "I like it when you arrive on time."

- **Negative Conditional.** "I am disappointed in the report you wrote."

- **Positive Unconditional.** "I think you are great."

- **Negative Unconditional.** "You are a waste of space."

Group/team examples:

- **Positive Conditional.** "You all work together to reach the target."

- **Negative Conditional.** "I am unhappy about the way you all giggled when our guest arrived."

- **Positive Unconditional.** "You are a great team."

- **Negative Unconditional.** "This team is underperforming."

Organization examples:

- **Positive Conditional.** "2019 was a year of growth and progress for the Smith firm. Smith achieved a series of key milestones in major programs of work, renewed and upgraded its product portfolio, and took important decisions to adapt and streamline its business."

- **Negative Conditional.** "The organization strives to comply with a Board of Directors' resolution that stated that the Board of Directors and senior executive team would be composed in a balanced way, in that it contains at least 30 percent women and at least 30 percent men. With the appointment of Ms Jones to the company's board of directors, the female representation on the board increased to 18 percent."

- **Positive Unconditional.** "You are a fantastic company."

- **Negative Unconditional.** "This company is appalling!"

You may notice that people also have their own rules about how they receive or do not receive and give or do not give recognition, asked for or did not ask for, and rejected or didn't reject. For example, I may not be able to give myself positive unconditional recognition. Alternatively, I may find that I cannot give negative conditional recognition, or I may accept negative unconditional recognition that others give me. Creating awareness of the way that you as a leader manage recognition in your everyday interactions will set the tone for the organization and the culture. It befits you to explore your personal patterns, which will give you more information on which to base your efforts if they are to be successful.

See Tool S4.1 on page 126, which provides a detailed understanding of the recognition patterns you are delivering.

4.3.3 Change, Change, Change

Change is a term that is in constant use these days, almost to the point where it has become overused. Change has always been there and has previously been the role of HR and similar others; the term is now widespread across all areas of an organization and a wide range of sectors. In recent years, the portfolio, program-of-work, and project management profession has adopted the term in abundance, initially to refer to activities relating to internal IT system roll-outs, but now referring to activities that are far reaching and organizationally transformational in scale.

There is much information and a fair bit of hype around change management. It seems to us that everybody wants it, but few really understand it. Indeed, with change it seems that everybody has a change management skill-set to offer. This is probably quite true; however, it is the deep understanding of change—that is, the need for the change, the scale and impact of the change, and the goal of the change—which differentiates the expert from the amateur.

What Is Change Management?

This question can be answered by sharing a quote from a whitepaper Iain previously wrote on change[*]:

> *Change management is a structured approach to transitioning individuals, teams, and organizations from a current state to a desired future state.*[†]

We like the clarity that this provides, because it hints strongly at the people aspects of change and change management.

We shall explore that further.

Types of Change

Having an intimate understanding of the nature of the change you wish to effect and the context in which you are working are critical to determining an appropriate change strategy and plan. Embarking on a change journey without some idea of the environment puts you at an immediate disadvantage. One of the first stages in planning change is to understand the type of change you wish to effect, where you want the organization to go, and how it plans to get there.

---

[*] Fraser, n.d.
[†] Fraser, 2014

Some examples of change include organizational structure change, merger and acquisition change, IT system release, business process re-engineering change, program-of-work change, and project scope change. All these present differing levels of risk and opportunity to the organization.

Not all changes will require the same level of planning or the same tools and techniques. As an example, simple change may affect many people, while complex change may only impact a small number of people. The level of change management effort therefore depends on two dimensions: the *complexity* of the change and the *scale* of the change. No matter what combination of these dimensions you intend to implement, there is always a degree of risk relating to the type of change.

There are three types of change that have varying levels of risk and therefore require different planning requirements.

- **Operational Change.** Tends to be changes to local processes and behaviors. Those tend to be departmental or localized and can be quite straightforward to implement with low risk levels.

- **Tactical Change.** Probably the most common type, as the business looks to continuously improve its performance and process efficiency, through organization-wide adjustments to everyday working methods and habits. Tactical change has moderate risk levels.

- **Strategic Change.** Often extreme or radical and usually requires the organization and its stakeholders to pursue a large shift from the current state. Transformation is the most extreme and far-reaching form of strategic change and can result in a future organization that differs significantly from the existing organization in terms of culture, structure, processes, and sometimes product or service offerings. Strategic change has high risk levels.

It is in the larger tactical and strategic change types that leading change is most needed. The quality of leadership could make or break the success of and long-term benefits to the organization. Larger changes can either be proactive (let's improve) or reactive (let's fight back). Sometimes it can be a combination of both. Today, though, it needs to be predominately proactive in order to stay ahead in a fast-changing world. Figure 4.1 shows different types of change and their relationship to impact and sustainability.

Four Conditions for Change

Successful organizational change occurs when the leaders convince employees to not only absorb the change, but to commit to it. This should be done via a

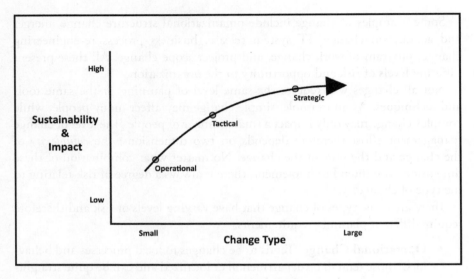

Figure 4.1 Change Types and Sustainability/Impact Relationship

change sponsor, usually an executive, and a change leader, the person managing the day-to-day change initiative.

To gain this commitment, all involved change leaders must strive toward achievement of the following:

- Actively model and advocate for the change.
- Provide surrounding structures, processes, and reward systems to support the change objective.
- Support people to see the point of the change, what it means for them, and agree with it. This may require a mindset shift.
- Develop people to have the skills to do what is required of them in the future.

People and Change

Organizational change is often difficult for staff and other stakeholders to accept. However, understanding why the change is happening and what it means for them personally can dramatically increase their receptiveness to the change. In addition, the confusion and fear experienced by staff during and after a major change event can be significantly reduced if the change is well planned, well communicated, and well led/managed.

Successful organizational change occurs when the change leaders have built rapport, gained trust, and influenced other people not only to absorb the change, but to commit to it (Fig. 4.2 indicates how this commitment can be influenced).

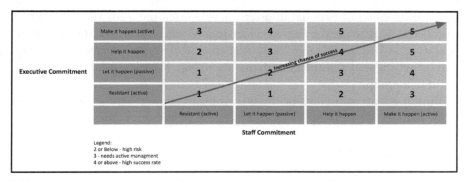

Figure 4.2 Assessing Change Commitment

Tribal Thinking—Throwing the Baby Out with the Bath Water!

When conditions change, leaders need to help people to be able to change their allegiance—more reason to pay attention to the material in Section 3. It helps leaders to know that people are being "difficult" for a good reason, and the work of the leader is to assist the culture, structure, and processes to work so the good people employed can do their work and achieve the purpose of the organization. In *Negotiating the Non-Negotiable*,* author Daniel Shapiro from the Harvard Program on Negotiation described the impact of how we identify with a group of people, often fiercely defending our group identity to the detriment and possible demise of us as a species on this planet. His experiments with workshop participants—world leaders, peacekeepers, CEOs of multinational organizations—all led to the same outcome: staying protective of their group or losing sight of the big picture of ultimate survival. What was especially interesting was that it was all based on a group that had only been formed for 55 minutes.

This is such important information for leaders of any group of people. It is especially important to consider the impact of this dynamic when we are forming and reforming teams and groups as part of modern agile, nimble, or matrixed organizations.

---

* Shapiro, 2017

Organizational Boundaries and Responding to Threat

Another interesting phenomenon that occurs as groups of people function together is how the strength of your group boundaries change with an external threat. That is, when there is a threat from outside the group, the boundaries between teams and sub-groups inside the main group become less rigid. For example, in times of national disasters, people often put aside their differences to collectively manage the recovery. Conversely, when teams within a group are operating as BAU, it is more likely that those differences between the groups will be highlighted and the boundaries are strong. It is clear who is in and who is out of a group.

Building your awareness of the way you can support strong boundaries or allow more fluidity can help in your change management endeavors.

Approaches to Change

Change management has evolved from being the domain of psychologists, HR people, and those "touchy feely" types, who seemed to talk about intangibles and at the same time lacked accountability, thereby hampering change management in becoming a recognized business discipline. The relatively recent emergence of professional bodies such as the Change Management Institute and similar others bears testament to that.

We both agree that people do the work in an organization—regardless of the advance of artificial intelligence (AI), people will always be the key to getting stuff done. Even if our sci-fi authors are suggesting that we will all be replaced by AI!

Recently, change management has experienced a paradigm shift away from the bolted-on "change consultant" model toward the creation of an integrated, structured approach that delivers tangible and measurable value to strategic as well as tactical business activity. Change management is seen by some as the application of two converging and predominant fields of thought: an engineering approach to improving business performance and a psychological approach to managing the human side of change. This convergence of thought from both the engineering and psychological fields of thought is seen as essential for successful business change in today's environment.

Forming an intimate understanding of the scope and scale of your planned change will guide you toward the most suitable approach or combination of approaches. The following approaches to change are common:

- **Engineering Approach**. This approach looks at how to make changes to the operations of a business as a mechanical system. It focuses on observable, measurable business elements that can be changed or improved. Historically, companies with a mechanical view do not value change management concepts. They do, however, value the result and the ongoing continuous improvement effort that is required.

- **Process Approach**. John Kotter has written widely on processes to use for change. His book *Leading Change*[*] outlines an actionable eight-step process for implementing successful transformations.

- **Psychological Approach**. The emphasis here is on how humans react to their environment and to change. This approach is concerned with helping everyone make sense of what the change means to them personally as well as collectively. The following three references are a selection of psychological approaches in common use today.

  o **Being vs Doing Approach**. In his book *Powerful Conversations: How High Impact Leaders Communicate*,[†] author Phil Harkins says that leaders influence cultural change not only through memos and meetings, but also through the many one-to-one conversations they hold throughout a day. What makes a conversation powerful is that all those involved share important feelings, ideas, and beliefs. Conversations must be planned and managed with the focus on "being the change," and the doing of the change will happen as a result.

  o **Skills-Based Approach.** Rosabeth Moss Kanter, in her book *The Enduring Skills of Change Leaders*,[‡] states that change-adept organizations share three attributes: the imagination to innovate; the professionalism to perform; and the openness to collaborate. The most important things a leader can bring to a changing organization are passion, conviction, and the ability to instill confidence in others. Too often, executives announce a change initiative, launch a task force, and then simply hope that people find the answers. Instead they should be offering a dream, stretching their horizons, and encouraging people to do the same.

  o **Storytelling Approach**. In her book *The Story Factor*,[§] Annette Simmons notes that stories make points in less confrontational ways than do arguments. By sharing a story, messages can be put out and left for the individual to ponder. Stories are powerful because they touch the

---

[*] Kotter, 1996

[†] Harkins, 1999

[‡] Kanter, 1999

[§] Simmons, 2006

120   The Business of People: Leadership for the Changing World

emotions as well as the mind in a memorable way. Changing a diametrically opposed opinion would require you to move in a "baby step" manner. A story gives you the powerful format to gradually and indirectly move someone from one end of a continuum to the other end.

The above is not intended to be a list from which you would select a single approach. In application, a combination of some of these approaches is likely. The combination will fluctuate as the phases of the change initiative are implemented and as staff commit to the change. Also, the type of change being considered will impact the choice of approach taken.

Often you will be seeking to change the habits of the organization. Remember in Section 1 we discussed how habits are formed and how they can be changed. Consider including that approach in your change plans and highlight the reward aspect of it. We believe that a psychological approach yields greater results because it relies on the human interface and communications aspects of people.

Change management is not a forgiving process. It must have a well-thought-out, clear objective and implementation plan. However, as you uncover more information and as assumptions and issues are challenged and resolved, you will need to revalidate ambiguities and demonstrate degrees of leadership courage in guiding and managing stakeholders to move forward. To us, the most successful change initiatives are those that have a plan that goes beyond the implementation mechanics of the change and that has a comprehensive view on how to sustain the change via people within the organization.

The Magic Ingredient?

It was tempting to create a list of magic ingredients, but we have decided to offer just one—but a very important one. It's the trait of *Leadership Courage*. To us, having this trait combats the notion of change leaders being too soft to succeed by not making decisions, or taking too long to make decisions, for fear of upsetting people.

There are several factors that differentiate the courageous and consistently successful change leader from those not so, and these revolve around the cultural and physiological make-up of the change leader. The ability to influence others is inherent within this.

Here are six questions to test your level of leadership courage:

- Do you make strong decisions even if they may upset some people?

- Do you readily provide constructive criticism?

Leading the Organization—Creating a Dynamic Organization   121

- Do you escalate to change sponsor or higher level?
- Do you demand excellence in the execution of the change program?
- Do you hold people accountable?
- Do you delegate rather than doing too much work yourself?

If you have answered "Yes" more than "No" to the above, you may already have good levels of leadership courage. While not scientific, your answers will provide a guide as to where you may wish to invest in some skill development. Change management is not for the faint of heart—it requires the head, heart, and gut (judgment) all to be present and aligned.

Footnote on Change

In summary then, there are three absolute focus areas that leaders and sponsors of change should prioritize. These are the *change need*, the *state of mind* within the organization (the climate), and the *change leader's capability*. It seems to us that many organizations put the change management process as the priority. No wonder there are failures!

Stakeholder management is also key to successful organizational change—program-of-work plans developed for the implementation of the change need to demonstrate an understanding of, and integration with, the approach taken toward the implementation of the change.

We need to be more receptive and welcoming of change and of the opportunities associated with risk as we strive to future-ready our organizations. As David Bowie sang back in 1971, "Turn and Face the Change."[*]

Enough said!

4.3.4 Organizational Agility

Agility is a word that is arguably overused today. In essence, it is about an organization's ability to be flexible or nimble, in its ability to conduct its ongoing business in a fast-changing environment.

Forward-thinking organizational leaders have recognized that post–global financial crisis (GFC) there is a greater need for organizations to be much more receptive to the delivery of value—that is, faster and for a cost that is the same or less than previous.

---

[*] Bowie, 1971

122 The Business of People: Leadership for the Changing World

Becoming a more agile organization requires a strong understanding of and line of sight on the organization's ability to plan, execute, and benefit from its goals and objectives. The use of balanced matrix type structures and the empowerment of people together with advanced use of portfolio management techniques continue to build momentum around the world.

Highly respected researchers and advisors McKinsey and Company,* in a recent survey output, stated that nine out of 10 executives, spanning all regions and sectors, ranked organizational agility as critical to business success and growing in importance.

Furthermore, the Economist Intelligence Unit[†] stated that nearly 90 percent of executives from their recent survey ranked organizational agility as *vital* for business success. They went on to state that 50 percent of CEOs agreed that rapid decision making and execution are *essential* to an organization's competitive advantage.

A third piece of research, this time by the Massachusetts Institute of Technology in the USA,[‡] suggests that agile organizations can grow revenue 37 percent faster and generate 30 percent higher profits than those that are not agile.

The bottom line here is that short-term nimbleness leads to longer-term resilience. Refer back to Section 1 for guidance on building resilience and optimism. You can apply those to the building of resilience and optimism among the people you lead.

4.3.5 Organizational Sustainability

The word *sustainability* seems at odds in the VUCA-impacted world, in which change and speed are the base ingredients of choice to conquer the volatile, uncertain, complex, and ambiguous world. Sustainability, in the context of leading the organization, is about a range of things that, when combined and nurtured, offer the organization a level of calm and resolve. This in turn makes people working in the organization feel good about themselves, their contribution, and in turn working for the brand.

So where do we start with sustainability? The answer lies in our ability to do a few things extremely well. Some of these will test your thinking and even challenge your learning. However, we are confident that pursuing them will allow you, as a leader, and your people to thrive day after day, month after month, and year after year.

---

* McKinsey & Co., 2006
† Economist Intelligence Unit, 2013
‡ Massachusetts Institute of Technology, 2012

Here are our top ten action areas, which are in no particular order:

1. Invest in culture and observe and evaluate climate.

2. Simplify the organization.

3. Adopt or adapt the philosophy of the 3P's to Success.

4. Use a value management framework to develop and implement strategy.

5. Be disciplined in your leadership principles, styles, and techniques.

6. Take time to scan, listen, and think.

7. Link vision and purpose statements. Communicate well.

8. Always be ready to change.

9. Be strong, be bold, but not foolish.

10. Encourage others always. Show the way.

We believe it is a case of repetition with adjustment as required. We would encourage you to apply these in an external and internal manner to form a sort of holistic environmental scan. By doing this, you should be well warned about any need for action associated with combatting the effects of the VUCA world. Deploying these action areas will greatly assist in building resilience within your people.

Leaders who want to project their organizations forward should be motivated by Project Management Institute (PMI®) research[*] that states that organizations with high levels of agility are twice as likely to see increased success with their new initiatives when compared to those with low agility. That can easily be considered a sustainable trait.

To get ahead, organizations must adapt and become more agile and nimble in today's environment. If the leaders are risk averse, then the organization is unlikely to thrive or even survive; conversely, taking too much risk can have the same effect. This presents a challenging dilemma for most leaders. Ultimately, the use of advanced techniques such as value-driven portfolio management and change management encourages leaders to empower and manage their people further and the organization to quickly adapt.

However, all the above will be weakened if corresponding investment in your people is ignored. Investment in people should revolve around three attributes of *technical skill, business management skill,* and *leadership skill.* An example of this is the PMI®, with its millions of stakeholders around the world. It has

---

[*] Project Management Institute, 2012

124 The Business of People: Leadership for the Changing World

recognized that its members and others in the project management field should develop their skills across those three attributes so that their leadership capability keeps pace with future needs. Indeed, their professional certifications require a balance of those skills to be attained and maintained over a defined cycle.

4.4 Case Study

A few years ago, Iain was on a speaking assignment in South Korea. The intended audiences were business oriented, and he had some local support in terms of language, administration, and logistics. There were three main engagements: the first with a newly formed not-for-profit organization where Iain was to present a keynote address; the second with Research & Development division of the giant Samsung organization at their splendid campus south of Seoul; and the third was with a large engineering and construction company.

The first two sessions went perfectly, and Iain could not fail to notice how gracious and polite everybody was. He was very motivated by that. The third session was to be in two parts, with the first an executive presentation to the CEO and leadership team in their corporate board room and the second a brief one-on-one session with the CEO himself. The first went very well, and despite the occasional language difficulty, good dialogue was had, and some keen questions were asked and answered.

The one-on-one with the CEO was also a success, albeit hard to gauge initially due to the short timeframe. Nevertheless, the CEO asked a few pertinent questions which, on reflection, Iain concluded that he asked privately rather than in front of his leadership team for fear of losing face—a not uncommon cultural trait in Southeast Asia. The CEO had a sense of humor though, and often smiled and offered a "one liner."

Iain recounts: "At the end of our session we were to go for lunch off-site to a fabulous restaurant that served traditional food in a traditional setting. As the CEO and I exited his office, we were met by some aides who were bowing initially and then fussing over the CEO and myself as we were ushered toward the elevator. On reaching the ground floor, we were met by more bowing people with huge smiles on their faces. Everybody seemed to know the CEO and showed their respect in the manner common to the culture of the country. In walking side by side with him, I was shown the same courtesy, as I was the CEO's guest and supposedly of equal status—quite flattering and certainly humbling! The CEO took time to speak, albeit briefly, to the reception team and to the driver of his car. At the restaurant, nobody ate until the CEO had tasted his food. Everybody, including me, had a drink because the CEO wished

Leading the Organization—Creating a Dynamic Organization 125

to have one, and some banter was had. People relaxed and chatted about business and the presentations."

The point to this case study disclosure is that, although the CEO clearly had huge amounts of legitimate power, he also showed traits of good leadership in his approach to each situation. A hierarchical people model is not a bad thing if good leadership traits are on display consistently and are genuine and sincere despite cultural norms.

Your future organization, especially if it grows, will require you to balance levels of diversity associated with race, age, sex, and culture. The smart leader will blend those into the organizational culture and make sure that they become authentic and real.

4.5 Tools

Tool S4.1: Recognition Profile Datasheet

Task:

1. Think about yesterday. Remember how your day began, then the middle of the day through to the afternoon and into the evening and night time.

2. Now, estimate how frequently you responded to each type of recognition.

Conditional		Gave		Didn't Give		Received		Didn't Receive		Asked for		Didn't Ask		Rejected		Didn't Reject	
10		+	−	+	−	+	−	+	−	+	−	+	−	+	−	+	−
0																	
		Gave		Didn't Give		Received		Didn't Receive		Asked for		Didn't Ask		Rejected		Didn't Reject	
0																	
10		+	−	+	−	+	−	+	−	+	−	+	−	+	−	+	−

Unconditional

Thanks to Julie Hay (TA Theorist)[*] for her thoughts about Recognition Patterns.

---

[*] Hay, 2009

Tool S4.2: Organization Assessment Questionnaire Sample

	Strongly Disagree	Disagree	Neither Agree nor Disagree	Agree	Strongly Agree	Not Applicable
LEADERSHIP *This section examines how your organization's senior leaders guide and sustain the organization through direction setting, demonstrated customer focus, and creating a high-performance environment. Also examined are your organization's governance systems together with its ethical, legal, and sustainable practices.*						
1. Senior leaders set a clear direction for the organization and communicate it effectively to all employees and relevant supply chains.						
2. The senior leaders are visible and accessible.						
3. The senior leaders demonstrate the organization's stated values, therefore modelling the behaviours expected of employees.						
CUSTOMER and MARKET FOCUS *This section examines how you determine customer and market requirements, expectations and preferences, and how your organization builds its relationship with customers, monitors their satisfaction, and develops future opportunities.*						
1. Information about current or potential customers and their products, services, and market requirements is continually gathered and used in all parts of the organization.						
2. There are processes in place to ensure that products and services are continually improved to meet customer and market requirements.						
STRATEGIC and BUSINESS PLANNING *This section examines how the organization develops overall direction and specific action plans, how objectives and actions are implemented and changed as required, and how progress is tracked and measured.*						

(continues on next page)

Tool S4.2: Organization Assessment Questionnaire Sample (cont.)

	Strongly Disagree	Disagree	Neither Agree nor Disagree	Agree	Strongly Agree	Not Applicable
1. There is a process for planning future strategic direction.						
2. Everyone has input or involvement at some stage in planning.						
PEOPLE FOCUS *This section examines how the organization enables people to develop and use their full potential in alignment with the organization's strategic direction and action plans. This includes building a culture that encourages performance excellence, full participation, as well as personal and organizational growth.*						
1. Work and jobs are designed so they contribute to employee cooperation, initiative, empowerment, and innovation.						
2. The characteristics and skills required from potential employees are identified, with new people recruited using this information.						
PERFORMANCE and KNOWLEDGE MANAGEMENT *This section examines organizational performance. It explores having a fact-based measurement system with the use of data and information (knowledge) to support key organizational activities, to make decisions based on fact, as well as to analyze the macro performance of the organization*						
1. The right information is collected and analyzed to determine overall organizational performance.						
2. The organization has processes in place to ensure accuracy, reliability, security, timeliness, and confidentiality of data, information, and knowledge.						

Tool S4.2: Organization Assessment Questionnaire Sample (cont.)

PROCESS MANAGEMENT *This section examines the way things are done to create customer and organizational value.* • Product and service processes include design, delivery, and operations. • Support processes for the organization's products and/or services— they can include financial and accounting, customer service, administration, sales and marketing, and information and knowledge management. *All processes, whether provided directly or through a supply chain, are designed with the customer in mind; they are aligned with strategic goals, are monitored against business objectives, and are continuously improved.*	Strongly Disagree	Disagree	Neither Agree nor Disagree	Agree	Strongly Agree	Not Applicable
1. The key processes for delivering customer value and organizational success are known and understood across the organization.						
2. Key product and service processes are designed to meet current and changing customer requirements.						

We would also like to have your feedback on what we do well, and on areas for improvement. Please take a few minutes to give us your views.

These are the three areas I think our organization does well:

1.
2.
3.

These are the three areas where I think our organization could improve:

1.
2.
3.

Tool S4.3: Stakeholder Categorization Guide Sample

Assessed Type	Definition	Management Actions
Advocates	Only group driving the change or initiative. Internal champions and sponsorship.	Active communications, keep regularly involved. Input to key milestones and decisions. Use for promotion of objectives and benefits.
Opponents	Have high understanding but low agreement to the initiative. Will potentially "lose out" in some way from the activity.	Initiate discussions and understand reasons for low acceptance. If the loss is perceived but not real, then convert using facts and data. Counter the reasons for low acceptance.
Indifferent	Individual or groups yet to take a definitive position on the initiative. Have a medium understanding and medium agreement.	Identify gaps in knowledge and seek to fill those. Seek their views on key issues and address concerns. Be careful not to make them opponents.
Blockers	Show resistance to the initiative or its aims, principally owing to having a low understanding and low level of agreement. This can be driven by: A lack of communication. A (perceived or actual) loss from the initiative. Knowledge of error in initiative assumptions.	Communicate proactively. Interview and meet. Explain and overcome fears. Use conflict management techniques. See views once understanding starts to develop.
Followers	Have a low understanding of the initiative aims and objectives. Support the initiative and tend to "go with the flow."	Increase their understanding for future benefit. Keep informed and positive. Avoid the temptation to exploit.

Leading the Organization—Creating a Dynamic Organization   131

Tool S4.4: Stakeholder Mapping Sample

Stakeholder (Group or Individual)	Impact	Importance/Influence	Position	AIH	LIH	HIH	MIH	Concerns	Actions

Legend: AIH = Against it Happening. LIH = Let it Happen. HIH = Help it Happen. MIH = Make it Happen

Tool S4.5: Communications Plan Sample

Name	Issue or Concern	Communication Objective(s)	Key Message(s)	Vehicle (medium)	Owner	Timing	Materials	Progress Notes

Epilogue

It is not the mountain we conquer, it is ourselves.
— Sir Edmund Hillary[*]

The Story Concludes

Sam has had a tremendous career path. He/she has redefined and created an organization that is sustainable, in terms of high performance, and is future ready. Sam has blended people together and invested in them. Furthermore, Sam has established that the core purpose of the organization must have a solid ethical base that supports the desired culture.

The ancient Scottish clan of the Lovat Frasers has a motto that was the rallying cry for clan gatherings and for battle. The use of the French language is a nod to the origins of the knights from north-west Europe, known today as Normandy in France, where some of the great Celtic tribes were based and apparently the Frasers originated. Leaders today could perhaps adopt and expand the rallying cry by the use of:

Je suis prest! (I am ready!) (The Lovat Fraser motto)

Êtes vous prêt? (Are you ready?)

Nous somme prêts! (We are ready!)

The best leaders will always find ways to give back as they focus more on what they give rather than what they get.

We began each section of the book with an epigraph that we felt was pertinent to the topics discussed in that section. The following are some

---

[*] Bonnie Louise Kuchler (2003) *That's Life : Wild Wit & Wisdom,* p. 20

134 The Business of People: Leadership for the Changing World

additional quotes from a selection of leaders from different geographies and sectors, and with different experiences. We think they are great, and we are sure you will also.

"Creating the right environment for your teams to succeed is fundamental not only to achieving your goals but also to attracting the right talent. Your people are your greatest asset and should be managed and looked after accordingly. They in turn will look after your business."

David Buisson, Executive Vice President, Metrolinx

"Leadership is not determined by structure. Values define good leaders. Good leaders are good people, strong communicators, motivators, and collaborative coaches. Above all good leaders are themselves."

Craig Bunyan, GM Technology, ANZ Banking Group

Leadership is the ultimate journey. As life-long learners, they teach, coach and mentor others and integrate emotional intelligence into their business and personal lives. Leaders are present in the moment, active listeners and make a difference in thousands of lives one conversation at a time. Seek out referent leaders and follow your passions. Helping others achieve their full potential is among life's greatest rewards. Enjoy the journey.

Scott Fass, CEO and Founder, Fass Advisory Group

"When leading, we must remember that we are but a part, it is impossible to lead from an 'ivory tower.' We must go deeper than just knowing, we must understand and to do so we must be engaged. Take time to understand every part of your responsibility, from the least experienced to the most trusted, from the shop floor to your board, from the least known to the person you see in the mirror. Only in doing so will you truly lead and, in doing so, you, your team, and the organisation will feel led and respond in kind. In short we must lead through life."

Lt Col (Ret'd) Stew Darling
Founder of the Lead through Life Framework

"Over the last 25 years of running global projects and teams, the greatest difference between success and failure was leadership. Teams that established open communication and trust with all stakeholders were able to deal with issues faster and get back on track. It all comes down to integrity (aka honoring your word), clear communication, and teamwork."

Scott Mairs, CEO, Blockchain Business Solutions.

"Leadership, like stewardship, is knowing when to play your hand and grasp the talents of others; and when to sit on it and allow others to play your hand for you. The dealer becomes life-long learning."

Dr Sarah Ross, Skema Business School & Other Institutions

"Before the culture can eat strategy for breakfast, the right leadership must be in place at all levels across teams and the organization. Driving decision tempo, knowledge, learning, collaboration, and trust across people and even technology as a teammate is a must for the future of work and disruption. It's all about the intangibles!"

Jordon Sims, Founding Partner, Imperium Global Advisors

We sincerely thank you for reading this book. We trust that our messages and stories will inspire your leadership journey and those of your people. We believe that the very best leaders always seek to improve their skills, their impact, and their giving. We encourage you to do also. Be bold, be courageous, be yourself, and above all, be good and kind to your people. He tangata, he tangata, he tangata.

Appendix: Poems to Ponder

Iain and Madeleine had several conversations on whether or not and where we would include the following poems within this book. We have done so here because we believe we all learn differently. Having a poem that can sum up our thoughts can provoke learning and understanding that a mere page of written words cannot. However you interpret them, enjoy them and take away what matters to you.

Relating to Section 1

I

I walk down the street.
There is a deep hole in the sidewalk,
I fall in.
I am lost . . . I am helpless.
It isn't my fault.
It takes me forever to find a way out.

II

I walk down the same street.
There is a deep hole in the sidewalk.
I pretend I don't see it.
I fall in again.
I can't believe I am in the same place
but, it isn't my fault.
It still takes a long time to get out.

138   The Business of People: Leadership for the Changing World

III
I walk down the same street.
There is a deep hole in the sidewalk.
I see it is there.
I still fall in . . . it's a habit.
my eyes are open
I know where I am.
It is my fault.
I get out immediately.

IV
I walk down the same street.
There is a deep hole in the sidewalk.
I walk around it.

V
I walk down another street.

"Autobiography in Five Short Chapters," © 1993, by Portia Nelson from the book *There's A Hole in My Sidewalk*. Reproduced with kind permission from Beyond Words Publishing, Hillsboro, OR.

Relating to Section 2

Emo-tion-ally
Em-pa-thy
Provides the connect-i-vi-ty
Between the leader and me
Shows the leader understands and shares what followers feel
Acknowledges followers' experiences as real
Leading with empathy is always important, but especially
When others are going through crisis, sadness or some atrocity
Empathetic leaders offer themselves authentically
Expressing true sentiment, avoiding hyperbole and hypocrisy
Everlast said, "God forbid you'd have to walk a mile in their shoes . . .
Then you'd really know what it's like to have to lose"
As a leader, you don't get to choose
When followers face challenges in life
You must be there to feel their strife

Be compassionate, feel followers' pain
Assure everyone the sun comes out after the rain
Leaders journey alongside while leading a support campaign
Inte-llect-u-ally
Em-pa-thy,
Is thinking NOT so easy to do
Leaders putting themselves in the place of you
Exemplary leaders think as…and take another's perspective
Recognize when they got it wrong, and are self-corrective
Empathy allows leaders to genuinely understand followers', listen to ideas with clarity
Removing personal bias is a leadership rarity
Make no mistake
To lead, you must partake
In the misery and suffering of those who have a stake
In the outcomes and benefits
Of those whom on the leader throne sits
Now, leaders need to get work done
And always being empathetic is necessary work, but un-fun
Think and feel outside of one's self, about more than number one
The takeaway
Of the day
Is that if a leader wants me to follow
Then often times that leader needs to swallow
Their pride
And hide
Their vanity
To feel what's inside of me.

Dr Bryan Deptula. Reproduced with permission bkdleaders.com/lead-with-empathy/

Relating to Section 3

We are connected
one to the other
by needs and hopes
that transcend infant groupings
so recently spawned
by divisive minds

140 The Business of People: Leadership for the Changing World

in this human cradle
from which we've still not
emerged with gentle strength
So we reach for dominance
and reach for advantage
to feel we deserve
a higher place than someone else . . . .
but we are connected
one to the other
with more in common
than we want to see,
for you need me
and I need you
connected as we are
in this cradle bed,
the same umbilical feeds us all,
when you draw breath
my lungs expand,
when I fall down
your body aches . . . .
we are connected
the one to the whole,
woven as art in search of a frame,
yet we seem to dwell
on the torn interruptions
ignoring the truth
that we are, connected.

"Connections" by Dudley Weeks; reproduced with permission of Dudley Weeks.

Relating to Section 4

I am an engineer
I need the facts
I need the measurements
How big is it?
How long will I live?
Will it hurt when I die?
How many more days can I work?

Can I still be the boss?
Can I control it or
Will it control me?
How many milligrams in this tablet?
Can I cry today?
I have the facts
I'm not an engineer
I'm a dying man
Can I now linger in your embrace?
Can I wipe away your tears?
Can I take the time to enjoy the beauty in;
My world?
My city?
And my room?
Can I allow you to wipe away my tears?
Must I blame them on the beautiful piece of music
Or can I accept that they are for all that might have been
Or all that was?
Is it true I have melted a little
Does it take something as evil as cancer
To shake up our "facts"
And mould them into feelings?
Feelings that were there
Just hidden beneath the preciseness
An engineer must exhibit
To hell with preciseness
Neatness
Schedules
Outcomes
(However, if someone could just tell me *where* this is going to happen I won't go
there till I've got everything done!)
My facts are becoming reality
They have their own timetable and
I must accept that my tendency to plan
May not make a great difference at the end of the day
Therefore,
Come, hold me tight
Keep me warm
Give me only the information for which I ask
My detail days are done

I need only lie back and enjoy the simplicity of
Your friendship
Your love
Your guidance
And your acceptance of me for who I am
A dying engineer.

"The Fact of the Matter," Mary Death, March 2002 (a poem honoring a dying engineer in his final days); reproduced with permission of Mary Death.

Glossary

Term	Description
Accountable	Personally responsible for an activity. Accountability cannot be delegated, unlike responsibility.
Agility	A term used to describe the degree of flexibility an organization has to combat change. Can also apply to a specific method of working.
Business value	A term used to express the entire value of an organization's business activity.
Change	Going from a current state environment to a desired future state.
Change management	The process of managing change from a current state toward a desired future state.
Corporate governance	The ongoing activity of setting and maintaining a sound system of direction and control by the directors and officers of an organization to ensure that effective management systems have been put in place to protect assets, earning capacity, related value, and the reputation of the organization.
Culture	A shared set of norms of organizational well-being that revolves around purpose, people, and performance.
Current state	Used in capability assessments or change initiatives. Describes the "as of now" status of the organization or group of people.
Ethics	A system of moral principles that affect how people make decisions and lead their lives. Ethics is concerned with what is good for individuals, organizations, and society and is also described as *moral philosophy*.

Future state	A forward-planned state of an organization, as planned by a change strategy.
Habit	Routine behaviors done on a regular basis. Habits are recurrent and often unconscious patterns of behavior and are acquired through frequent repetition.
Leadership	The skill that allows one to influence others toward an objective or goal.
Leadership courage	A set of attributes that a good leader displays and uses in various combinations to drive decision making, problem solving, and work guidance.
Management	The organization and coordination of the people and activities of a business in order to achieve defined objectives.
Matrix structures	Designs for an organization's structures that allow for great cross-functional work to be done via delegated levels of leadership.
Neuroleadership	Neuroleadership is the application of science-based findings from neuroscience to the field of leadership.
Nimbleness	*See* Agility.
Overindulgence	A term used to describe a human condition often applied to children who have had parental experiences in which the child is free to act as though he/she is the center of the universe.
Responsibility	Used to describe a person who has permission and is expected to deliver outputs associated with programs of work and projects. Responsibility can be delegated.
Stakeholder	An individual, group, or organization that may affect, be affected by, or perceive itself to be affected by a decision, activity, or outcome of an initiative.
Strategic goals	Somewhat aspirational views on mid- to long-term desired position for an organization. Subset of organizational strategy. Can apply to individuals as well.
Sustainable	A term used to describe an organization that can cope with any fast-changing situation by adjusting its business model quickly and with low stress. A form of protection from the future.
Transactional Analysis (TA)	A model of understanding human communication and interaction.
Talent management	Defined policy and mechanisms that consider, seek, recruit, develop, and retain people for the organization.
Transformational	A term used to indicate a significantly sized strategic change initiative that is often organization wide.

Values 1—Personal	A collection of traits that an individual displays and lives by in all circumstances. This is often the core of the person's psychology.
Values 2—Organizational	A collection of traits that the organization states that guides the overarching behavior of each staff member in a similar manner and thereby the organization as a whole. These values are often integrated into a cultural statement.
VUCA	An acronym for Volatile, Uncertain, Complex, Ambiguous. Term often used to describe a fast-changing world reality.

Bibliography and References

Argyris, C., Putnam, R., and McLain Smith, D. (1985). *Action Science, Concepts, Methods, and Skills for Research and Intervention.* San Francisco, CA: Jossey-Bass. Action Design.

Berne, E. (2016a). *The Games People Play: The Psychology of Human Relationships.* London, UK: Penguin Life.

Berne, E. (2016b). *Transactional Analysis in Psychotherapy: A Systematic Individual and Social Psychiatry.* Pickle Partners Publishing.

Bowie, D. (1971). Changes.

Choy, A. (1990). The Winners Triangle. *Transactional Analysis Journal,* 20(1), 40–46.

Clarke, J., Dawson, C., and Bredehoft, D. *How Much Is Too Much?* (2014). Boston, MA: Da Capo Lifelong Books, Revised edition.

Conran-Liew, T. (2004). *Working in a Group.* Auckland, NZ: Playcentre Publications.

Death, M. (2002). *Private Collection.* Unpublished.

Dearlove, D. (2003). *The Ultimate Book of Business Thinking.* Oxford, UK: John Wiley and Sons Ltd.

Deutschman, A. (2007). *Change or Die.* New York, NY: Harper Collins.

Duhigg, C. (2014). *The Power of Habit.* New York, NY: Random House.

Dweck, C. (n.d.) Decades of Scientific Research That Started a Mindset Revolution. Accessible at https://www.mindsetworks.com/science/

Eckman, P. (2019). The Atlas of Emotions. Accessible at www.atlasofemotions.org

Economist Intelligence Unit. (2013). *Why Good Strategies Fail: Lessons from the C-Suite*. London, UK: The Economist Intelligence Unit.

Faisandier, J. (2009). *Thriving Under Fire: Turn Difficult Customers into Business Success*. Landfall, NZ: Steele Roberts.

Fisher, R. and Brown, S. (1989). *Getting Together*. London, UK: Century Hutchinson.

Fraser, I. (n.d.) Whitepaper accessible at www.jacobite.co.nz

Fraser, I. (2014). The War for Talent Is On: Are You Strategically Prepared? Proceedings from PMI® PMO® Symposium, Miami, FL. Newtown Square, PA: Project Management Instutite.

Fraser, I. (2017). *The Business of Portfolio Management—Boosting Organizational Value*. Newtown Square, PA: Project Management Institute.

Gilman, S. (2005). *Good Boundaries Set You Free*. TEDxSnoIsleLibraries. Accessible at www.youtube.com/watch?v=rtsHUeKnkC8

Goal QPC. *Memory Jogger* series of books. Accessible at www.goalqpc.com

Goleman, D. (2000). Leadership That Gets Results. *Harvard Business Review,* March–April: pp. 1–11.

Goleman, D. (2007). *Emotional Intelligence—Why It Can Matter More Than IQ*. New York, NY: Random House.

Goleman, D. (2012). Social Skills and EQ. Accessible at http://www.danielgoleman. info/social-skills-and-eq/

Goleman, D. (2013). Empathy-101. Accessible at http://www.danielgoleman.info/ empathy-101.

Harkins, P. (1999). *Powerful Conversations: How High Impact Leaders Communicate*. New York, NY: McGraw Hill.

Hay, J. (1995). *Transformational mentoring*. London, UK: Sherwood Publishing.

Hay, J. (2009). *Transactional Analysis for Trainers,* Chapter 5. Broadoak End, UK: Sherwood Publishing.

Hay, J. and Tucker, A. (2010). *Steps to Success*. Self-Published Tool.

Hayakawa, S. I. (1939). Language in Thought and Action. Harcourt. ISBN: 970-0-15-648240-0.

Heifetz, R. and Linsky, M. (2002). *Leadership on the Line: Staying Alive Through the Dangers of Leading.* Boston, MA: Harvard Business School Press.

Herrmann International Group. Whole Brain® Thinking Model. Accessible at www.hbdi.com

Hunter, D., Thorpe, S., Brown, H., and Bailey, A. (2007). *The Art of Facilitation— The Essentials for Leading Great Meetings and Creating Group Synergy.* Aukland, NZ: Random House.

Kahler, T. (1975). Drivers: The Key to the Process of Scripts. *Transactional Analysis Bulletin* (5)3, July. doi: 10.1177/036215377500500318

Kanter, R. (1999). The enduring skills of change leaders. *Leader to Leader 13, Harvard Business Review.* pp. 1–6. (Reprinted in *Ivy Journal*, May–June, 2000).

Karpman, S. (1968). Fairy Tales and Script Drama Analysis. *Transactional Analysis Bulletin,* 7(26), 39–43.

Kotter, J. (1997, 2012). *The Leadership Factor.* New York, NY: Free Press.

Lencioni, P. (2002). *Five Dysfunctions of a Team: A Leadership Fable.* Hoboken, NJ: Jossey-Bass.

Massachusetts Institute of Technology. (2012). Organizational Agility. PMI® *Pulse of the Profession®*, p. 4.

Maxwell, J. (1998, 2007). *The 21 Irrefutable Laws of Leadership.* Nashville, TN: Thomas Nelson.

McIntosh, G. and Rima, S. (1997, 2007). *Overcoming the Dark Side of Leadership.* Grand Rapids, MI: Baker Books.

McKinsey & Co. (2006). Building a Nimble Organization: A McKinsey Global Survey. *McKinsey Quarterly.* Accessible at mckinseyquarterly.com.

Mountain, A. and Davidson, C. (2015). *Working Together. Organisational Transactional Analysis and Business Performance.* Burlington, MA: Gower Publishing.

Nelson, P. (1993). *There's a Hole in My Sidewalk.* Hillsboro, OR: Beyond Words Publishing.

O'Neill, H. (2013). What We Don't Understand About Trust. Accessible at https://www.ted.com/talks/onora_o_neill_what_we_don_t_understand_about_trust

Pranis, K. (2017a). *The Keeper's Handbook.* Saint Paul, MN: Living Justice Press.

150   The Business of People: Leadership for the Changing World

Pranis, K. (2017b) *Circle Leader's Handbook*. Accessible at www.livingjusticepress. org/vertical/sites/%7B4A259EDB-E3E8-47CD-8728-0553C080A1B0%7D/ uploads/Circle_Keeper_Handbook_2017.pdf.

Porath, C. (2019). Civility in the Workplace: Self-Assessment. Accessible at http:// www.christineporath.com/assess-yourself/.

Project Management Institute. (2006). Code of Ethics and Professional Conduct.

Project Management Institute. (2010). *PMI® Talent Triangle™*. Newtown Square, PA: Project Management Institute.

Project Management Institute. (2012). *Pulse of the Profession®. In-depth Report: Organizational Agility*. Newtown Square, PA: Project Management Institute.

Project Management Institute. (2015). *PMI® Thought Leadership Series. Delivering on Strategy: The Power of Project Portfolio Management*. Newtown Square, PA: Project Management Institute.

Raven, B. H. and French, J. (1959). The Bases of Social Power. In D. Cartwright (Ed.), *Studies in Social Power,* pp. 150–167. Ann Arbor, MI: Institute for Social Research.

Rock, D. (2009). Managing with the Brain in Mind. *Strategy in Business,* (56) Autumn, Reprint No. 09206 2009.

Rozin, P. and Richter, C. (1976). The Complete Psychobiologist. In E. M. Blass (Ed.), *The Psychobiology of C. Richter,* pp. *xv–xxviii*. Baltimore, MD: York Press, 1976.

Sanborn, M. (2006). *You Don't Need a Title to Be a Leader*. Colorado Springs, CO: WaterBrook Press.

Shapiro, D. (2007). *Negotiating the Non Negotiable: How to Resolve Your Most Emotionally Charged Conflicts*. New York, NY: Penguin Books.

Simmons, A. (2006). *The Story Factor* (2nd edition). New York, NY: Perseus Book Group.

Singleman, G. and Swan, H. (2013). Article from a Radio New Zealand interview. Accessible at https://www.radionz.co.nz/national/programmes/ninetonoon/ audio/2568201/glen-singleman-and-heather-swan-base-jumping

Stewart, I. and Joines, V. (2002). *TA Today: A New Introduction to Transactional Analysis*. Nottingham and Chapel Hill, UK: Lifespace Publishing.

Stewart, J. (1984) The Role of Information in Public Accountability. In: A. Hopwood and C. Thompkins (Eds.) *Issues in Public Sector Accounting.* Oxford, UK: Philip Allen Publishers Limited, 13–34.

Stone, D., Patton, B., and Heen, S. (1999). *Difficult Conversations—How to Discuss What Matters Most.* Penguin Books; Anniversary, Updated edition (November 2, 2010), p. 8.

Thomas, K. and Kilmann, R. (2009–2019). Thomas-Kilmann Conflict Mode Instrument Model. Accessible at www.kilmanndiagnostics.com

Tuckman, B. (1965). Developmental Sequence in Small Groups. *Psychological Bulletin* (63).

Tuckman, B. and Jensen, M. (1977). Stages of small group development revisited. *Group and Organization Studies* (2)4, 419–427.

Tudor, K. (2008). "Take it": A Sixth Driver. *Transactional Analysis Journal,* (38)1, 43–57.

Venezky, E. and Slawuta, P. (2014). *Hack Your Brain: Secrets of an Elite Manhattan Tutor.* CreateSpace Independent Publishing Platform (1819).

Index

A
ambiguity, 20, 21, 98, 105
amygdala hijack, 5, 6, 47
assertiveness, 4, 22–25, 36, 92, 93

B
boundaries, 12, 14, 21, 36, 40, 64, 87, 118

C
changes, 1, 2, 5, 6, 14–26, 31, 40, 43, 47–49, 56–63, 68, 73–76, 85, 91, 106–123, 127, 130
climate, 106, 110, 111, 121, 123
complexity, 20, 72, 105, 115
core concerns, 5
culture, 44, 49, 51, 54, 61, 75, 76, 81, 83, 89, 99, 106–117, 123–125, 128

D
destructive thinking, 17, 18
discounting, 19

E
ethics, 8, 9, 21, 65, 106, 112

F
feelings, 2, 4, 5, 7, 9, 10, 13, 14, 17, 18, 25–29, 39–42, 52–55, 59, 67, 68, 74, 75, 91, 96, 98, 119
focus, 1–3, 7, 9, 16, 22–24, 27, 39–42, 45, 48, 50, 61, 72, 75–78, 89, 91, 99, 107–111, 119, 121, 127, 128
frame of reference, 7, 8, 17, 19, 47, 48, 51, 69

H
habits, 10, 12, 15–18, 21, 23, 26, 84, 115, 120

I
influence, 8, 22, 31, 34, 41, 43, 53, 55, 64, 82, 83, 109–112, 117–120, 131

L

leadership courage, 21, 49, 120, 121
learning states, 11, 12
learning styles, 12, 30, 31, 102

O

optimism, 4, 21–23, 122
overindulgence, 38, 56, 89, 108, 110

P

people, 2, 3, 6–13, 16, 21–23, 32, 34,
    38–51, 54–78, 83, 84, 87–125, 128
personal values, 8
portfolio management, 8, 37, 43, 71,
    106, 108, 122, 123
principles, 8, 9, 34, 43, 50, 65, 83,
    109, 123

R

resilience, 1, 7, 21, 22, 98, 122, 123

S

scripts, 2, 3, 27, 47, 69, 112
self-care, 64
sustainable, 33, 47, 81, 97, 109, 110,
    123, 127

T

techniques, 2, 6–10, 14, 32, 40–43,
    51, 52, 69, 72, 83, 90, 95,
    106–109, 115, 122, 123, 130
thinking styles, 9, 11, 55, 83, 101,
    102
trust, 21, 25, 26, 34, 37–40, 43–51,
    61–64, 73–77, 82, 88, 94–97,
    107, 109, 117

U

uncertainty, 20, 21, 43, 105, 109

V

values, 5, 8, 9, 14, 21, 27, 34, 35, 43,
    55, 59, 65, 68, 72, 83, 88, 89,
    99–111, 118, 119, 122, 123,
    127, 129
volatility, 20, 105
VUCA, 1, 8, 11, 20, 21, 51, 83, 105,
    107, 110, 111, 122, 123
vulnerability, 3, 13, 44, 87

W

working styles, 12, 13, 32, 33, 89,
    96